Norman T. Carrington MA

Brodie's Notes on William Shakespeare's

The Merchant of Venice

Pan Educational London and Sydney

First published 1945 by James Brodie Ltd,
15 Queen Square, Bath BAI 2HW
This edition published 1976 by Pan Books Ltd,
Cavaye Place, London SW10 9PG
All rights reserved
ISBN 0 330 50015 5
Printed and bound in Great Britain by
Richard Clay (The Chaucer Press) Ltd, Bungay, Suffolk

CONTENTS

	PAGE
THE AUTHOR	5
THE PLAY—	
Plot	8
Structure	9
Setting	10
Atmosphere	12
Characters	13
Style	28
THE ELIZABETHAN THEATRE	31
THE TEXT OF SHAKESPEARE'S PLAYS	36
TEXTUAL NOTES AND REVISION QUESTIONS	38
QUESTIONS	77
PASSAGES SUGGESTED FOR MEMORISING	84

THE MERCHANT OF VENICE

THE AUTHOR

SURPRISINGLY little is known of the life of our greatest dramatist, and the little we know is derived mainly from brief references to his name in legal and other formal documents. He was born in Stratford-on-Avon, and although the exact date of his birth is unknown, there is a record that he was christened William on 26th April, 1564, the third child of John Shakespeare, a man variously described as glover, wool-dealer, farmer, and butcher. Until about the year 1578, when his business seems to have begun to decline, John Shakespeare was a notable figure in Stratford, and it is probable that William was educated at Stratford Grammar School, where he may have learned the "small Latin and less Greek" for which Jonson gave him credit. However this may be, the next thing we know that can be accepted as reliable is that at the end of 1582, at the age of eighteen, he married Anne Hathaway, a woman eight years older than himself, and that by 1585 three children had been born of the marriage. In this year he is thought to have left Stratford for London. Tradition has it that his departure was owing to trouble over deer-stealing in the grounds of Sir Thomas Lucy, but in the light of modern research it would appear that he left with a band of strolling players, the Queen's Players, who visited Stratford in 1585.

Whether his wife and children ever lived with him in London is not known, but it is unlikely; nor do we know what he himself did there before 1592, but from a pamphlet published in that year by Robert Greene, we have news of him as actor and playwright. Plague caused the theatres to be closed in 1593, and on their re-opening in the following year we know that Shakespeare was a member of the Lord Chamberlain's Company (known, after the accession of James I, as the King's Men), and it is probable that he stayed with this company for the remainder of his career, writing plays for it and acting with it in various theatres. His connection with the company must have brought him considerable financial reward, for we know that in 1596 his father, presumably aided by his successful son, applied to the College of Heralds for the right to assume a family coat of arms, and in the following year the playwright purchased (for £60!) New Place, one of the largest houses in Stratford. Although the house is no longer there, the foundations can be seen and the garden is open to the public. As his fortunes prospered, Shakespeare bought shares in two theatres, the Globe, built in 1599, and the Blackfriars, built in 1609, so that, in addition to his pay as actor and writer, he would receive his share of the profits on these investments.

Thus, in 1611, when still under fifty years of age, Shakespeare retired to his native town, a fairly wealthy man, though he seems to have kept up a connection with London, as he was concerned in a legal dispute over the purchase of a house in Blackfriars in 1615. He died in Stratford-on-Avon, survived by his wife and two daughters, on 23rd April, 1616, and was buried in the Parish Church, where thousands of people from all over the world visit his grave every year.

As an actor Shakespeare does not seem to have been eminent, but even in his own day his fame as a dramatist was very great. Thus Meres, in 1598, described him as "the most excellent in both kinds" (*i.e.* in comedy and in tragedy), and even Ben Jonson, whose dramatic work was in a very different vein from that of Shakespeare, remarks in his *Discoveries*, "I lov'd the man and do honour his memory (on this side idolatry) as much as any".

Shakespeare probably began his work as a dramatist by collaborating with others and patching up old plays which his company wished to revive. His first completely original play is believed to be *Love's Labour's Lost* (1591?), though the date of each play is itself a problem, since the dates are not given in the First Folio (the first collected edition of his plays, 1623). His non-dramatic works consist of two narrative poems, *Venus and Adonis* (1593) and *The Rape of Lucrece* (1594), and the one hundred and fifty-four sonnets published in 1609—without Shakespeare's permission it is thought. The first one hundred and twenty-six of the sonnets are addressed to a young man, the poet's friend and patron, the remainder to a "dark lady", and the identity of neither of these two is established, nor is it decided how far, if at all, the series may be considered auto-biographical. Most of Shakespeare's plays were written for performance in the public playhouses, and they were conveniently classified in the First Folio in three groups—comedies, histories and tragedies. But when considered chronologically they seem to fall naturally into four periods, thus admirably described by Professor Dowden.

First, from about 1590 to 1595-6, years of dramatic apprenticeship and experiment; secondly, from about 1595-6 to about 1600-1, the period of the English historical plays and the mirthful and joyous comedies; thirdly, from 1601 to about 1608, the period of grave or bitter comedies and of the great tragedies; last, from about 1608 to 1611 or 1613, the period of the romantic plays which are at once grave and glad, serene and beautiful.

Professor Dowden names these periods respectively "In the workshop", "In the world", "Out of the depths", "On the heights". All the evidence points to 1596 or 1597 as the date of the composition of *The Merchant of Venice*. Thus it belongs to the second period, though it does not fit in to either of Professor Dowden's categories—it is neither a historical play nor, in spite of the happy ending, a mirthful and joyous comedy, in fact it barely escapes a tragic climax through Shylock's hatred, and it seems to be only by a twist at the end that Shakespeare gives it a happy ending.

The Merchant of Venice is a popular play and is often played. Students unable to see a live performance may like to know that there is a recording (a straight reproduction) on sale.

THE PLAY

PLOT

Portia, a rich lady of Belmont, can be won in marriage only by the man who chooses from three caskets the one which contains her portrait.

Bassanio wishes to try his fortune, but is short of cash, and so asks to borrow three thousand ducats from his friend Antonio in order to equip himself well and make a good show before Portia. Though Antonio is a very rich merchant, he happens to be short of ready money at the time, as all his capital is locked up in merchandise at sea. But his credit is good, and he borrows the three thousand ducats for three months from the Jewish money-lender Shylock. Shylock, who really hates all Christians, affects to be willing to lend the money free of interest out of good-will, and suggests a "merry bond" under which Antonio shall forfeit a pound of his flesh if the debt is not repaid within the three months. Bassanio half protests against Antonio's signing such a bond for him, but Antonio brushes aside his misgiving and puts his seal to it.

At Belmont Bassanio chooses the right casket. Portia accepts him as her husband and gives him a ring which he swears never to part with. But in the very hour of Bassanio's triumph comes news that Antonio's ships have been wrecked, that the bond is forfeit, and that Shylock is pressing for the penalty laid down in it, and that Antonio is in prison awaiting trial. Shylock's hatred has been made more intense by the fact that his only daughter has eloped with Lorenzo, a Christian and a friend of Bassanio and Antonio, and has robbed him of the money and jewels she could lay her hands on. Portia is all sympathy for the friend of her husband-elect and authorises Bassanio to pay the debt three-fold if necessary to secure his release. Bassanio sets off at once for Venice.

Shylock rejects all appeals for mercy and refuses any offer of money-payment, standing on the penalty of his bond. The case comes to trial, and owing to its unusual nature the Duke has sent for a learned doctor of laws to try it. The doctor is unable to attend through illness, however, and in his absence recommends a deputy, who is really Portia in disguise. Portia adds her appeal to the Jew to accept thrice the money and show mercy. He again refuses whereupon she confounds him by interpreting the bond more literally than even he thought possible. Shylock leaves the court a broken man. Portia declines a fee for her services, but begs the ring she had given Bassanio. He refuses it at first, but, pressed by Antonio, sends it after her.

When Portia and Bassanio meet again at Belmont, Portia mischievously accuses Bassanio of giving the ring away to a woman (which was indeed the case), and after Bassanio's denials and explanations she confuses him by producing the ring, which also proves to him that it was she who was the judge at the trial.

STRUCTURE

There are two main plots and two sub-plots in *The Merchant of Venice*.

Main plots.   1. The Bond-plot—Antonio's escape from Shylock's revenge.

             2. The Caskets-plot—Bassanio's winning of Portia.

Sub-plots.   1. The Lorenzo-Jessica plot—the elopement of Shylock's daughter with Lorenzo and her robbing of her father.

             2. The Rings-plot—the giving away of their rings by Bassanio and Gratiano.

Contrast is a fundamental principle of Shakespearian drama. Here the bitter hatred of Shylock in the Bond-plot is set off against the love of Bassanio and Portia in the Caskets-plot, and also the subordinate lovers Lorenzo and Jessica and Gratiano and Nerissa. The student should notice the disposition of the scenes of the main and sub-plots.

The Caskets-plot develops faster than the tragic plot. The success of Bassanio's quest is settled in Act III, Sc. ii, whereas the climax of the Bond-plot is not reached until Act IV, Sc. i.

The different strands are well bound together, otherwise the play would be "broken-backed" and fall apart into two (if not four) separate plays. The two main plots particularly are firmly dovetailed into one another. Antonio becomes Shylock's victim through making possible Bassanio's marriage with Portia. Shylock's hatred against Antonio is inflamed by his daughter's elopement with a Christian. It is Portia who saves Antonio. Lorenzo and Jessica benefit from her sentence upon Shylock. Portia's ring was first given to Bassanio (and Nerissa's to Gratiano) immediately after his choice of the right casket (the climax of the Caskets-plot), and they gave them away immediately after Antonio's rescue (the climax of the Bond-plot). Characters from all four plots meet in the final act. The chief binding link is Bassanio, who is the friend of Antonio (Bond-plot), and who becomes the husband of Portia (Caskets-plot). But even a minor character like Launcelot has no inconsiderable part to play in linking together the different strands. First of all he is the servant of Shylock, then of Bassanio, he acts as message-bearer between Lorenzo and Jessica (including the letter with plans for their elopement) and, finally, he appears at Portia's house at Belmont. It might be thought that a complex web like this would make a play confusing and difficult to follow, but not when the different threads are woven together in such an interrelated pattern.

The student would do well to make a list of the characters which appear (1) in any single plot, (2) in more than one plot.

Other comments on the interlacing of these different plots and the contrasts produced between them will be found on pp. 38, 42, 57, 58, 64-5 and 72-3.

SETTING

The great majority of Shakespeare's plays, apart from the English Histories, are set in places abroad, a device which of itself gave them a romantic colouring.

The local colour of all Shakespeare's plays is that of Elizabethan England, whether the story is one of Italy, Denmark or Scotland, and in whatever age. Nowadays we should demand strict accuracy in scenery, costume and topical references, but then, for playwright and audience alike, the life and spirit of a play mattered more than strict accuracy in local colour. "It is the spirit which giveth life." People saw in the drama a reflection of their own life and experience; its appeal was in no wise analytical or educational, but human. (See also the topicality of the play, below.)

Further, in those days people were untravelled and uneducated, and anachronisms would not strike a false note in an age more familiar with the stories than with their settings.

And it must be remembered that there was no scenery and no period costume. Incongruities which would become apparent beside "realistic" scenery would not be noticed then. In references to a character's dress it would be farcical were the references historically correct but to something the character was not actually wearing on the stage!

The Merchant of Venice takes place nominally in or near Venice, but we are really never very far from the London Shakespeare knew. Venice, an independent state, is spoken of as an English city with a right to administer justice under a royal charter (III. ii, IV. i). There are references to doublet and hose (I. ii), and a hit against the use of cosmetics and the fashion of wearing false golden hair (III. ii)— a constant subject of satire at a time when dark hair was very unfashionable (see note on "golden", p. 60). Gentlemen wear their hats at dinner (II. ii), masques (with torchbearers) enliven a party (II. iv), wedding rings and knives are inscribed with "posies" (V. i) and an hour-glass is a common method of. telling the time (I. i). But more important than all these specific allusions in giving an Elizabethan flavour to the play is the utter abhorrence with which usury is regarded—the view-point of the "man-in-the-street" of Shakespeare's day. In the Middle Ages the Church expressly forbade usury to Christians (indeed it was prohibited by Act of Parliament as late as 1552) so the Jews were not slow to take up their chance, and thus usury became a practice with which Jews were identified. Money-lenders have never been very popular, and here was an additional source of hatred for the Jews. But the play was immediately topical too. It was written not long after the public hanging and disembowelling of the Jew Dr.

Lopez, falsely convicted on a charge of trying to poison Queen Elizabeth I, and Shakespeare's audience would have spurned a Jew, even as Antonio did. But it was Shakespeare's triumph also to show how Christians in the play denied common humanity to a man because he was a Jew.

In *The Merchant of Venice*, however, Shakespeare has paid more attention to accurate local colour than is usual with him. The carrying-trade of Venice between East and West ("the trade and profit of the city consisteth of all nations") is continually brought home to us, and we are made to realise the city's place among the waters by Bassanio's voyage to Belmont and Portia's in the other direction on "the tranect", "the common ferry which trades to Venice". The Doge himself appears in the play, the rich merchants meet on the Rialto (IV. i), where the chief topic of conversation is the news of their argosies at sea (I. iii, and III. i), Lorenzo and Jessica escape in a gondola (II. viii), and Old Gobbo brings a present of a dish of doves for Bassanio (II. ii). But by far the most realistic touch is speaking of England as if it were a foreign country (I. ii, II. viii, III. i), especially the last of these, with its casual and dramatic "the Goodwins, *I think they call the place*".

ATMOSPHERE

In the First Folio *The Merchant of Venice* was classed as a comedy. It is a comedy only in so far as it turns out happily for the lovers and for Antonio. The very first line of the play strikes a note of depression (see p. 38) which deepens as the play proceeds. The atmosphere often verges on tragedy, in fact Shylock is a great tragic figure, too powerful for the atmosphere which surrounds him. Even when the peril of his enmity has passed we can scarcely say we are happy, the peril has been too grim for that; there is no room for anything but sober thankfulness and a grave relief. For a time the dark hatred of the malignant Shylock has cast a cloud over the happiness of the lovers, but the cloud is lifted when the scene shifts to the moonlit avenue at Belmont, and we forget Shylock when we see Jessica in the arms of her lover waiting to welcome home Portia and Bassanio. Together in one play we have great power, deep feeling, rare beauty, sportive gaiety and happy romance. The plot cannot be classified in a formula, any more than life itself can be. Here we have something better than a play written to fit a pattern, we have a page of the book of life, and when we read that book it is worth reading. Shakespeare's art is not bound down by the technical regulations of the schools; he strives to create a form for himself in which he may represent neither comedy nor tragedy alone but human life.

The beautiful poetry and picturesque language of the play, which give it so much of its charm, are dealt with under "Style" (pp. 28-30).

CHARACTERS

Shakespeare's plots are often careless and improbable, and the idea of Portia carrying off a disguise in an official position in a court of law is rather thin, to say the least. Shakespeare's great artistic power is in characterisation, and through it a story which in inferior hands would be crude and improbable becomes real and lifelike. Given these circumstances the characters act like real people—we should know them if we met them in the street. Characterisation bears the same relation to plot as architecture to bricks and mortar. We are moved by any story in so far as we feel our kinship with the actors. A story with a "realistic" plot has no life if the characters are wooden, but a crude plot becomes alive when living people inform it.

Shylock

The villain Jew.

Shylock stands out in all literature a great figure. Although the play takes its title from Antonio, Shylock is the central character and into him Shakespeare has thrown his whole strength. He makes a profound impression— even Portia is a slight character by his side.

A usurer, with a lust for gold, he is the soul of avarice, yet the keynote of his character is not avarice, but hatred. His heart is like a stone. His hatred outruns his avarice in the trial scene when he is offered thrice the money and prefers Antonio's life. But even here avarice may impel his hatred, for had Shylock not said, "Were he out of Venice,

I can make what merchandise I will"? He hates Antonio on two main counts.

> I hate him for he is a Christian;
> But *more*, for that in low simplicity
> He lends out money gratis.

In Act III, Scene i, he repeats these causes of his hatred to Salanio.

But Shylock is a product of racial persecution and his "Christian" foes have had much to do with making him what he is. Antonio, the best of the Venetians (*i.e.* the English), does not deny that he has called Shylock "misbeliever, cut-throat dog, and spit upon his Jewish gaberdine", and tells him plainly,

> I am as like to call thee so again,
> To spit on thee again, to spurn thee too.

There is obviously some truth in the way Shylock views his Christian enemies. Their oppression has made him bitter and revengeful, so that when he gets a chance of taking action against the persecutors of himself and his race he takes it up eagerly and will not let it go. "Sufferance", he says, "is the badge of all our tribe", and his hatred is all the fiercer for having been repressed and denied expression for so long. "Shylock," says Charles Lamb, "is, in the midst of his savage purpose, *a man*. His motives, feelings and resentments have something human in them." This is just the chance he has been waiting for, the million-in-one chance that he had hardly dared to hope for when he cunningly plotted Antonio's death under a show of friendship, and now—"I will have the heart of him, if he forfeit". He realises that in ability and intelligence he has no equal among his Christian foes. His keen intellect and great resource and self-reliance have been fostered by his life apart as an outcast among men—he has *had* to depend on himself, for who would go out of his way to help the Jew? He knows his capabilities, yet he finds himself always spurned by the Christians as an inferior creation. Little wonder that he has become embittered; all the world is against him through no fault of his own, and he accepts the world as his enemy. His hand is against every man. Now he will show them how he alone can set himself against the lot of them, and make *them* sue to *him* for a mercy they themselves never show. His appeal to Salarino in Act III, Scene i, is unanswerable.

Hath not a Jew eyes? hath not a Jew hands, organs, dimensions, senses, affections, passions? fed with the same food, hurt with the same weapons, subject to the same diseases, healed by the same means, warmed and cooled by the same winter and summer, as a Christian is? If you prick us, do we not bleed? if you tickle us, do we not laugh? if you poison us, do we not die? and if you wrong us, shall we not revenge?

Equally unanswerable is Shylock in the trial scene. Neither the Duke nor Bassanio can refute his arguments. He replies in cruel words, yet they are not wholly unjustified, and holds his Christian foes to scorn, laying bare their faults. As to their opinion of his action he is quite unconcerned; he has been an outcast from society for as long as he can remember, so that society's opinion of him does not enter into it.

One of the most admirable traits in Shylock is his staunch loyalty to his race and religion. Perhaps this is another result of persecution, for history tells us that religious oppression generally has the opposite effect from that intended. Those who are persecuted for their faith find that they have something to cherish and keep alive, and a faith which in more comfortable days they would let slip becomes vital. In the play Shylock utters powerful and eloquent pleas, not for his *own* rights, but for the rights of his despised race, and his patriotism and religious earnestness give dignity to his character. His hatred of Antonio is made more intense by Antonio's attitude to his race and religion—"He hates our sacred nation." "Cursed be my tribe if I forgive him." His enmity to Antonio thus becomes a point of national honour.

A sudden sign of tenderness in Shylock comes as a surprise. Jessica had stolen a valuable ring from him. "Thou torturest me, Tubal," says Shylock, hearing how Jessica had exchanged this ring for a monkey, "it was my turquoise; I had it of Leah when I was a bachelor." Shakespeare's villains are always human, not melodramatic monsters, and even Shylock treasures the memory of a dead wife. His home affairs show another side to his character. It has been urged that there was justification in Jessica's flight because Shylock was cruel to her. Shylock may have been too bound up with the world to have had time for her, and he speaks to her no tender word, but there is no sign of cruelty. It does not follow because a father does not understand his daughter that he does not love her. Yet, truly enough, Jessica could say, "Our house is hell" (and Launcelot had much the same notion—II. ii). Shylock apparently kept her indoors away from participation in the amusements of other girls lest "the sound of shallow foppery enter my sober house", and no doubt he gave her scanty pocket-money from his store of riches. Much has been made of Shylock's words to Tubal, "I would my daughter were dead at my foot, and the jewels in her ear! Would she were hearsed at my foot, and the ducats in her coffin!" But I do not think that this, spoken in a moment of passion, can be taken literally, any more than Bassanio's words spoken under the stress of the situation in court, when he expresses his willingness to sacrifice his wife to "this devil" in order to deliver Antonio. There is no doubt that Shylock feels his daughter's loss. If he had no love for her, her loss would not have affected him so much (nor, incidentally, have increased his enmity towards Antonio). He trusts her in a way he did no one else, handing his keys over to her safe-keeping. Such implicit trust speaks some affection.

But when we have said all we can for Shylock we must admit that his punishment is not undeserved. It certainly was not Shakespeare's conception that Shylock was "more sinned against than sinning". Portia's plea for mercy is one of the most beautiful things in literature. How could Shylock resist it? Yet it falls on deaf ears. He rejects it to put his knife in his enemy's heart. Just at the moment when success seems in his grasp, he is defeated by his own weapon—the letter of the law. His fate is terrible— especially the forced conversion (that is, judged by modern standards), and our hearts cannot help but be touched by his suffering. We are glad Antonio is free, yet we are not glad Shylock is treated so. The shock has been too much for him, and when in court he feels unwell and asks leave to go home, we know that if Shakespeare had worked the tragedy to the bitter end Shylock has gone home to die. He is vicious, cunning, avaricious, cruel and heartless, a terrible figure of a man; he is without a friend (even Tubal seems to take a malicious delight in "torturing" him), without a soul to speak a good word for him, and the boys of Venice mock him in the streets; yet a pathos clings about him to the end. Shakespeare exhibits the ordinary Elizabethan prejudice against the Jew; but in the soul of his soul, despite the thoroughness of his English nationalism, he knew the heart of the stranger (see also p. 21). Shakespeare makes us see Shylock not only as the other characters see him, but as he sees himself. This vision and insight make the character of Shylock what it is.

Portia

> The poor rude world
> Hath not her fellow.

"What shall I say," wrote John Ruskin, "of . . . the calmly devoted wisdom of the 'unlessoned girl' who appears among the helplessness, the blindness, and the vindictive passions of men, as a gentle angel, to save merely by her presence, and defeat the worst intensities of crime by her smile?"

The charm of Portia's character defies analysis. She is possessed of all the graces—is rich, beautiful, clever and honourable. When we first meet her we are struck by her sprightly intellect and keen wit as she playfully runs her suitors over. Yet her satire is never bitter and vituperative like Shylock's.

The way she sticks to the rigid terms of her father's will in her choice of a husband shows her strong sense of honour, duty and loyalty to her father's memory. Honour counts more with her than love, and she might well join with Richard Lovelace,

> I could not love thee, Dear, so much,
> Loved I not Honour more.

"I could teach you how to choose right, but then I am forsworn," she says to Bassanio, though she may have authorised a hint to be given him as to which casket to choose (see note on "So", p. 59). There are many small touches which lead us to think of Portia as a sincere, religious and devout woman (e.g. I. ii), and not least her famous speech on the quality of mercy. Before her suitors she shows a proper dignity, stateliness and pride. She lets Morocco and Arragon do most of the talking, yet we are made to feel her presence, and this very fact emphasises her reserve.

With her servants Portia is free and easy, but she has been brought up to command, and we feel all the time that they "know their place" and would not take liberties, though not so much through fear as the respect they bear their mistress.

Her superiority to Bassanio is unquestionable. She, in her modesty, is the only one who does not see it, and as soon as she realises she is to become his wife she disparages herself by the side of him as "an unlesson'd girl, unschool'd, unpractised". She is genuinely modest and does not affect modesty to be contradicted. She never thinks of how anything affects *herself*. As soon as she hears of the predicament of Bassanio's friend, although he is quite unknown to her and she might very well say that Bassanio's bachelor friendships were no concern of hers, she offers the amount of the loan "twenty times over" to secure his release. There is no trace of jealousy in her make-up: she never thinks of Antonio as a rival for Bassanio's affection. She is quite willing to lose her husband, even on their wedding-day, since his errand is an errand of mercy.

To offer cash might be an easy way for one in Portia's position to discharge her husband's obligation to Antonio, but Portia refuses to let matters drop there, and cannot rest while there is a stone unturned to save him. With what a girlish zest she relishes disguising herself as a "bragging Jack"! Yet this girlish zest is accompanied by a strongly practical grasp of the situation. So far she has been acting according to the terms of her father's will; now the crisis brings out her own initiative and strength of purpose. She makes her decisions quickly and is prompt to act upon them.

> Waste no time in words,
> But get thee gone.

She shows some self-confidence in never wavering, and she carries through her plan with assurance and poise. Without this assurance she would have been undone, for one slip would have meant discovery. She sees the funny side of the adventure, too (III. iv. 60-78), and this, no doubt, contributes to her poise. Yet we are never allowed to forget that Portia is a woman. With what womanly tenderness she tries to win Shylock over by appealing to his better nature! Three times she seeks to persuade him of his own free will to do good rather than force him (offering him at the same time thrice his principal), knowing all the time that she holds the trump card in her hand. Then, when he has proved adamant to all entreaty, including her beautiful and earnest speech on "the quality of mercy", with swift strokes she turns the tables on him. In her character tenderness unites with strength.

Her sense of humour does not desert her in the most serious moments, and when Bassanio has said he would sacrifice his wife to deliver Antonio we can imagine the twinkle in her eye as she comments,

> Your wife would give you little thanks for that,
> If she were by, to hear you make the offer.

She is not annoyed with Bassanio for putting her second, her sense of humour saves her from self-conceit and helps her to see the situation aright without false sentiment. Her love of a practical joke is seen in the ring episode which follows. But in everything she shows a sense of proportion, and she does not carry the joke too far. Antonio naturally feels uncomfortable as the cause of Portia's annoyance with Bassanio for parting with her ring—"I am the unhappy subject of these quarrels". "Sir, grieve not you," says Portia, "you are welcome notwithstanding", and she soon brings the episode to a close. Portia is the soul of courtesy and would not willingly hurt anyone, not even the self-opinionated Prince of Arragon. And overlying all her qualities is a sound common-sense, that virtue which keeps the whole world steady. Bassanio is indeed lucky to have won such a woman for his wife.

Dramatically Portia is a contrast to Shylock. She is young, he is old; she is generous, he is mean (though in fairness to Shylock it must be said that he was only trying to amass the wealth which Portia's father had amassed for her); she is gracious, he is snarling; everyone speaks well of her, everyone speaks ill of Shylock.

Antonio

A kinder gentleman treads not the earth.

Antonio's noble qualities impress everybody. His is a small speaking part, yet we get to know him well from the tributes of those who come into contact with him. Perhaps the dramatic reason for these many tributes is to build up a character who has so small a part (only some 180 lines). Bassanio, who is indebted for much to him, naturally thinks him

> The kindest man,
> The best-condition'd and unwearied spirit
> In doing courtesies.

This testimony is echoed by all the others (except, of course, Shylock). "I love thee," says Gratiano, "and it is my love that speaks." Salanio refers to him as

The good Antonio, the honest Antonio—O, that I had a title good enough to keep his name company!

Lorenzo says "How true a gentleman" he is, and that before Antonio has recommended him for half Shylock's fortune. The people of Venice, high and low, respect him. "Twenty merchants, the duke himself, and the magnificoes of greatest port" make special efforts to persuade Shylock to relent, the Duke takes "great pains" to "qualify" Shylock's "rigorous course", and his very gaoler gives him special privileges—"so fond to come abroad with him at his request".

The chief reason for Shylock's hatred of him is his magnanimity in lending money gratis, and furthermore he had redeemed debtors who had fallen into Shylock's clutches. Antonio is always ready to help anybody in trouble. And to kindly deeds he adds a gracious personality. Perhaps it was this trait which led Shylock to speak of him as "fawning" and "smug".

From the beginning Antonio takes life rather seriously.

> In sooth, I know not why I am so sad:
> It wearies me.

Salanio speaks of Antonio's "embraced heaviness", as if he felt it was almost a pose. Antonio's is a grave, melancholy nature. It seems clear, however, that Antonio had not always been like this, else why were his friends so concerned about him? Further, he himself says that he has "much ado to know himself". But whatever his disposition, he shows great strength of character, and when death stares him in the face he meets it with a calm and patient resignation. Here, above all, we see the lengths to which his utter unselfishness will go. During the strain of the trial he never even once so much as *hints* that it was Bassanio's fault, and when sentence is about to be pronounced he passes over the ordeal which awaits him lightly with a pun, saying that he is ready to repay Bassanio's debt "with all his heart". Then, the issue of the trial over and his life spared, his first thought is for Lorenzo and Jessica, and he even asks the Duke to remit that part of Shylock's penalty which should go to the state.

This last must have cost Antonio something when we consider his treatment of Shylock elsewhere. Long before Shylock plotted against him Antonio seemed to take a pride in spurning Shylock and treating him in public with rudeness and contempt (see p. 14). It is difficult to reconcile this discourtesy with the rest of his character. One would imagine such a man would instinctively shrink from insulting *anybody* so grossly, but Antonio seems proud of it and tells Shylock that he will probably abuse him again, "spit on him again, and spurn him, too". When Shylock shows a seeming kindness to Antonio he takes it as a sign that "The Hebrew will turn Christian: he grows kind". Kindness in a Jew is something beyond Antonio's conception. However, suffering does something to mellow his attitude to the Jew, and, facing Shylock in court, with the sympathy of the court on his side, he insults him no longer, "But," says he, "I do oppose my patience to his fury." When sentence has been pronounced against Shylock, it is ironical the way Antonio thinks he has given way to a burst of Christian generosity in asking for more favourable terms for Shylock with the proviso that "he presently become a Christian". But we should not expect Shakespeare to take a leap forward into our own age and make the people in his play look upon a Jew as we would. Antonio's uncharitableness towards a Jewish usurer is the outlook of the ordinary Christian of Shakespeare's time, and how else can Shakespeare present life except as he sees it? Nothing could better have made us realise the nation's intolerance of a Jewish minority than such persistent insult from no less a person than the Merchant of Venice.

At the end, when we are told that Antonio's ships have unexpectedly come safe home, we have ceased to be interested in his fortunes. This was a concession to popular taste demanding a "happy ending" all round.

Bassanio

Of all men . . . the best deserving a fair lady.

At the outset Bassanio appears as a reckless and extravagant fortune-hunter. In financial difficulties, through living above his income, he wants to borrow money to improve his chances of marrying a wealthy heiress, and when he has married her he will be able to pay off this debt and previous ones out of her money! He sets off to marry Portia under false pretences. That he does admire her is unquestionable (see his last speech in Act I, Sc. i), but in describing Portia to Antonio the first thing that comes to his mind is that she is "richly left". In his favour it can be said that he puts his position honestly before Antonio, without excuses and without pretence. Incidentally, Bassanio did not need three thousand ducats to win Portia; there was no clause in her father's will debarring a poor man choosing rightly. Still, Bassanio may not have known all the conditions, and, in any case, had Portia not been favourably impressed by him, she would not have given him the hint.

Bassanio is a better judge of character than Antonio, and in his distrust of Shylock would "rather dwell in his necessity" than have Antonio's "seal to such a bond", though he has no grounds for supposing that Antonio will be unable to re-pay his debt. "I like not fair terms and a villain's mind" is his final comment on the bargain.

We get a better picture of Bassanio from what his friends say about him than from what he does himself. Antonio, we are told, "only loves the world for him". Gratiano "must" go with him to Belmont, and will not be denied, and undertakes to "put on a sober habit" for the privilege. Launcelot Gobbo considers his service a vast improvement upon Shylock's, but perhaps this is not to be wondered at.

Those who know him speak of him and to him with respect. Salanio refers to him as Antonio's "most noble kinsman", and Lorenzo addresses him as "My Lord Bassanio". Nerissa considers this scholar and soldier worth her encouragement, and the impression left with Portia after Bassanio's one visit is that he is "worthy of thy praise". The woman who had been wooed by suitors from the four corners of the earth wishes that she could be

> trebled twenty times myself;
> A thousand times more fair, ten thousand times more rich;
> That, only to stand high in your account,
> I might in virtues, beauties, livings, friends,
> Exceed account.

The best that can be said for Bassanio is that Portia is proud to be his wife.

Gratiano

Let me play the fool.

Gratiano is hearty and lively, one of the hail-fellow-well-met type, a good mixer, the sort of man who makes any party go with a swing, but who gets on your nerves, maybe, when you have to live with him day after day. "Gratiano speaks an infinite deal of nothing, more than any man in all Venice", says Bassanio, and takes the precaution of making him promise "to allay with some cold drops of modesty his skipping spirit", to prevent his making "faux pas" and letting him down in front of Portia, a promise which Gratiano faithfully kept, in fact he did not speak once at Belmont (except aside to Nerissa) until after Bassanio's choice of the right casket, and then only to announce his own good fortune in love. For himself, Bassanio regards Gratiano as excellent company and encourages him to have his fling at the bachelor party.

> *Gratiano.*   Nay, but I bar to-night: you shall not gauge me
> By what we do to-night.
> *Bassanio*   No, that were pity:
> I would entreat you rather to put on
> Your boldest suit of mirth, for we have friends
> That purpose merriment.

Naturally, such a man regards Antonio's "sadness" as a dreary flop and tries to do something to liven him up.   A chatterbox perhaps he is, but not an *empty* chatterbox, and one capable of real affection for his friends and in due course for his wife. Gratiano greets every situation with a merry word, and is something like Launcelot, only with more refinement. Even in the court he delights in making Shylock eat his own words by his witty retaliation, "O upright judge!—Mark, Jew:—O learned judge!" His language is picturesque and his images are very apt and pointed, and there is some shrewd sense in some of his longer speeches (*e.g.* I. i. 79-104 and II. vi. 8-19).

The chatterbox of the play has the last word (see p. 72), but if we could be taken farther maybe he would not always be in that position. At home Nerissa's tongue would be a good match for him.

Nerissa

This fair one here.

As a maid Nerissa takes a subordinate place to her mistress; Portia naturally takes the initiative. Nerissa is the same type of character, in a lower social position. Her wit is as playful, and at the same time she is capable of "good sentences, and well pronounced". She takes her part in Portia's scheme to rescue Antonio as capably as Portia takes hers. She enjoys a practical joke and enters into the rings joke with zest. She is devoted to Portia, and agrees to tie up her life with Gratiano only on condition that Portia too is won by Bassanio. She bears no malice at being called "a little scrubbed boy", in fact rathers enjoys it, as would appear from her rejoinder to Gratiano,

> And pardon me, my gentle Gratiano;
> For that same scrubbed boy, the doctor's clerk,
> Did give me this.

We leave her feeling that she will be quite equal to the task of keeping Gratiano in order.

Jessica

Most beautiful pagan.

"Wise, fair, and true," says Lorenzo of Jessica. We will not quarrel with him that she is fair. Although she strikes us as too much of a girl to be called wise, yet left to herself in Shylock's house she has developed considerable self-reliance and takes the lead over Lorenzo and makes the plans for their elopement. "She hath directed how I shall take her from her father's house," admits Lorenzo. But true? At the moment Lorenzo says, "And true she is, as she hath proved herself", she has just thrown him a casket of stolen jewels, and jewels stolen when she was left in a position of trust with her father's keys. As a lover, pre-occupied with his own affairs, Lorenzo may mean true only *to him*. To her father Jessica told a direct lie (II. v. 45). Jessica disclaimed being "her father's child", but in her coveting of her father's jewels and her successful well worked out deception of him she showed herself very much "her father's child". Nevertheless, she did not want the jewels to *hoard*, and, as often happens with misers' children, due to natural revulsion against their parents' hoarding, she had no conception of the value of money and squandered money and jewels recklessly once she had them—"fourscore ducats at a sitting", and exchanged a turquoise ring (did she know it was her mother's gift to her father?) for a monkey. There was none of her father's avarice in Jessica—one cannot imagine Shylock giving a ducat to Launcelot.

Jessica leaves her father for good and all without a touch of remorse.

> Farewell; and if my fortune be not crost,
> I have a father, you a daughter lost.

Shylock had made life very dull for her, cooped up behind his shutters, but one would like to think that even while she rejoiced in Lorenzo as a deliverer she yet had a thought for the father who had brought her up and loved her beyond any other living person. Apparently Jessica's mother had died when she was too young to remember her, and the fact that she has no woman to turn to makes her life harder and increases the pathos of her situation.

She shows none of her father's national and religious consciousness. It is not as an act of will, the result of a considered judgment, that she renounces her religion. The only thing that matters is that she is in love, and Lorenzo's religion does not enter into her thoughts—it would have been all the same had he been a Mohammedan.

Perhaps when the first flush of freedom had worn off Jessica would become less irresponsible and more dependable. Although she has seen so little of the world, she can move in the world with propriety. She is not a pushing, forward girl. She knows her place at Belmont and says little when Portia is present, and she is quite shy of appearing before Lorenzo "transformed to a boy". She shows no envy of one who outshines her and is generous in her praise of Portia (III. v). Portia, a good judge of character, regards her as a capable woman and trusts her (jointly with her husband) with the management of her house in her absence, apparently with no cause for regret. (Did Portia, however, know that when she was left in charge of her father's house she robbed him and ran away?) Jessica is practical and, at the same time, is not without imagination. One would never think of connecting Shylock with poetry, but although, like Shylock, Jessica says she does not like music, she has an imaginative temperament, as the opening to Act V alone would show us, and she will find encouragement for this side of her nature in Lorenzo. Jessica is a passionate southern beauty, more alluring, but less attractive, than either Portia or Nerissa.

Fate deals kindly with Jessica. While Shylock gets all the punishment, she gets less than she deserves. We are without Portia's opinion on how *she* would stand before the law for robbing her father. Instead of receiving punishment, she is further rewarded, and is assured of the rest of her father's fortune on his death. But whatever her faults, we never think of Jessica as evil, simply as thoughtless. As she says herself,

> Love is blind, and lovers cannot see
> The pretty follies that themselves commit.

And it is primarily as a lover that she appears in the play.

Dramatically her part throws light on another side of Shylock's life—his home life, as opposed to his business life, and she is a link between the two main plots by running away from Shylock to be seen again at Portia's house at Belmont.

Lorenzo

Lorenzo, and thy love.

Lorenzo is devoted to Jessica, and her love is the only thing he considers important. He is of an imaginative temperament, an impression which Shakespeare gives by putting into his mouth some of the finest poetry in the play (*e.g.* V. 54-65). He is fond of music and more poetical than Jessica (*e.g.* V. 83-8). Portia considers him highly and on a very short acquaintance hands over the charge of her house to him, though from the way he leaves the planning of their elopement to Jessica it would appear that she had the better head for "directing".

The dramatic function of Lorenzo and Jessica in the construction of the play is to provide a pair of more romantic and glamorous lovers as a contrast to the graver pair, Bassanio and Portia, and secondarily to the more sprightly and less passionate pair, Gratiano and Nerissa.

Launcelot Gobbo

A merry devil.

Launcelot Gobbo, in the First Folio consistently called the clown of the piece, is the counterpart of Gratiano in a lower walk of life. He is full of sheer animal spirits, fond of a practical joke and of wilfully misinterpreting people's words, he fancies himself as a maker of puns and he can be quite witty on occasion (*e.g.* III. V). Though he tricks his "sand-blind" father, he does it good-humouredly without ill-feeling or malice, and from his father's opinion of him we gather that he has made a good son. He imagines himself as "young *Master* Launcelot" and tries to act the part by decking out his conversation with long words and learned expressions, with the result that it becomes a hotch-potch of malapropisms and Latin tags.

Launcelot makes life more endurable for Jessica and robs her father's house "of some taste of tediousness". Even Shylock likes him, notwithstanding he is a Christian—"The patch is kind enough". He is perfectly trustworthy, and Jessica commits to him her love-letters to Lorenzo. Though he and his father bungle their approach to Bassanio when Launcelot seeks service under him, Bassanio takes to him immediately and orders that he be given "a livery more guarded than his fellows", which would no doubt please Launcelot mightily. Not the least surprised to hear this praise of him would be Launcelot himself.

Dramatically Launcelot plays a not unimportant part. He provides a link between the two main plots by leaving Shylock's service for Bassanio's, he acts as messenger between Lorenzo and Jessica, he gives another side-light on Shylock's home life, he comes between the main characters so that when they re-appear we have an impression of the flight of time (III. v), and everywhere he provides comic relief.

STYLE

Professor Dowden has an excellent summary of the development of Shakespeare's style.

In the earliest plays the language is sometimes as it were a dress put upon the thought—a dress ornamented with superfluous care; the idea is at times hardly sufficient to fill out the language in which it is put; in the middle plays (*Julius Cæsar* serves as an example) there seems a perfect balance and equality between the thought and its expression. In the latest plays this balance is disturbed by the preponderance or excess of the ideas over the means of giving them utterance. The sentences are close-packed; there are "rapid and abrupt turnings of thought, so quick that language can hardly follow fast enough; impatient activity of intellect and fancy, which, having once disclosed an idea, cannot wait to work it orderly out"; "the language is sometimes alive with imagery".

The Merchant of Venice is one of the middle plays.

There is much beautiful poetry in *The Merchant of Venice* and many passages are worth committing to memory. Such a passage is Lorenzo's speech which opens Act V, or, a little later on, his beautiful description of the moonlight, or Portia's famous tribute to mercy.

Graphic and figurative language abounds, and the richness and vividness of the imagery is to be noted. The similes and metaphors have that sense of surprise and yet of fitness which characterises the imagery of a genius. It never occurs to us that there is anything exceptional about the expression—it seems the only way. Such a line as "How sweet the moonlight sleeps upon this bank" is marvellous in its simplicity, and we wonder how it comes to be so beautiful. Notice the number of monosyllables in this line and in the other speech of Lorenzo referred to above. We also see the power of simple language in many of Shylock's speeches, or in Portia's when she is delivering judgment (IV. i. 303-10 and 322-30). Sometimes a simile or metaphor is extended beyond the original point of the comparison, as, for instance, in III. ii. 24-8 and 53-62.

Many expressions in the play have "caught on" and become household words, enriching our language apart from their restricted application in the play. Such a one is Shylock's approval of Portia's support of his claim at first—"A Daniel come to judgment!"

There are fashions in literature as in everything else. A pun has been defined as "the lowest form of wit", but in Elizabethan times punning was extremely popular. Portia enjoys puns just as much as the people "below-stairs" (I. ii), and Gratiano does not think it unseemly to pun in court. The double meaning is generally quite obvious, but in cases of difficulty owing to changes in the language an explanation is given in the notes.

Use of Prose

The normal form in Shakespeare's plays is blank verse. When prose is used it is for a definite purpose.

Prose is invariably used for

1. Comic characters (*e.g.* Launcelot Gobbo) and

2. Characters of lower social position (*e.g.* Nerissa).

This was a literary convention at a time when literature was aristocratic and the chief characters in plays (as in life) were kings and nobles. Scenes in which the lower orders of society figure are a contrast; these people live on a lower plane of feeling than the main characters, and thereby emphasise the height of the feeling of the main characters, and the contrast in the medium of expression—prose instead of verse—is in perfect keeping.

3. Letters, formal addresses, etc. (*e.g.* Bellario's letter, IV. i).

There is not a great deal of prose in *The Merchant of Venice*, but all the changes from verse to prose and prose to verse should be carefully studied and reasons for them sought. In Act I, Sc. ii prose is the medium not only because Portia is talking with a servant—this servant can herself speak in verse when her love for Gratiano is the theme—but also because it is a free and easy, homely scene. Principal characters talk in prose when they express a lower level of feeling than that in which their characters are cast as a whole. Notice how in Act I, Sc. iii prose is the medium when Bassanio and Shylock are discussing the bargain, but when Antonio, who is to suffer, enters, the level of feeling is raised to a higher pitch and there is a natural transition to verse. Further, at this point Shylock's pent-up hatred is stirred by the sight of the "fawning publican". In Act II, Sc. ii Bassanio speaks with Launcelot and Old Gobbo in prose, but as soon as they have gone out he turns to verse: similarly Lorenzo, when he turns from Launcelot to Jessica in Act III, Sc. v. In his rage Shylock speaks in prose in Act III, Sc. i. Prose, especially the crisp, staccato prose Shylock uses here, expresses his distracted state of mind much better than verse, which would be too beautiful, smooth and regular for the expression of rage which makes Shylock almost speechless. In this crisis of his life Shylock's prose is terrifying. The passage beginning, "Hath not a Jew eyes?" shows how Shakespeare can write prose with as much power as verse; it is, indeed, one of the finest passages in the play. Here is the spontaneous outburst of a repressed emotion, welling up from the depths of a wronged soul. It is on the border line between prose and poetry, a species of prose-poetry, without a regular rhythm but charged with a rhythmic flow, like the waves of the sea. The short rhythmic clauses are linked together by parallelism or balance corresponding in form and sense, like the poetry of the Old Testament.

Shakespeare shows complete mastery of his style and diction. They are equally suited to the dignified scenes between Portia and Bassanio, the passionate scenes between Lorenzo and Jessica, the scenes envenomed by Shylock's insatiable hatred and the comic scenes between lesser characters. Finally, there are no ups and downs, there is one high level of excellence.

THE ELIZABETHAN THEATRE

AT the time of Shakespeare there were probably not more than five public theatres in the land, all in London, and they were built according to the design of the inn-yards of the period, which had been found marvellously convenient places for the presentation of plays.

The theatre was circular or octagonal in shape. The main part of the auditorium was the large round pit, open to the sky, in which the poorer people *stood* (the "groundlings"). Encircling this, round the walls, were three balconies, covered on top but not in front (like the "stands" on a football ground) and containing seats. The price of admission to the pit was one penny, equivalent to at least two shillings nowadays, and balcony seats ranged from twopence to half a crown, according to their position. When it was wet the performance was postponed until the next day.

The stage was large, jutting far into the pit, and was without scenery and any but the most meagre properties. Hence it made no difference that people stood at the side of the stage as well as in front. The scenery was created in the imagination of the audience by the words of the characters in the play: it was made part of the play, so as not to obtrude and destroy the illusion of reality, as, for example, in *The Merchant of Venice*, V. 54. The play, would be performed in broad daylight. Act V happens by moonlight. Practically every character refers to the moonlight, and thus, by little natural touches, the audience is constantly made aware of the setting. Lorenzo refers to it ll. 1, 54 and 66, Jessica 6, Nerissa 92, Portia 109 and 124, Gratiano 142 and Bassanio 220. In addition there are several references to the fact that it is night-time (*e.g.* ll. 1-25, 89, 100 and 128).

The play went straight on without intervals. Lack of intervals and frequent changes of scene were immaterial when the stage was without scenery, consequently a succession of short scenes as in Act II, is quite common in Elizabethan drama. It should be remembered that on Shakespeare's stage there were no separate scenes *as such*. In the early part of the present century his plays were presented with elaborate, often spectacular, scenery, and sometimes the audience would become impatient at the constant delays while it was being changed. At the present time there is a return to a simple stage setting, in keeping with that of Shakespeare's day, as, for instance, at the Royal Shakespeare Theatre, Stratford-on-Avon. There is good reason

to believe that when they were first produced the plays took considerably less time than they do today. The Prologue to *Romeo and Juliet*, for example, refers to "the two hours' traffic of our stage".

The end of a scene was frequently marked by rhyming lines, as in Act I, Scenes i, ii (at the end of a scene in prose) and iii. Just as the scenery had to be *put into* the words of the play, so had entrances and exits to be arranged as *part of* the play. In a modern play an actor can get into position before the rise of the curtain, but on the open stage it would seem artificial if he walked on and then started his first speech, or finished the scene and then walked off. Such endings as I. i, "Go, presently inquire, and so will I"; I. ii, "Come, Nerissa.—Sirrah, go before", clear the stage and at the same time fit in perfectly naturally with the action of the play. In fact, in *The Merchant of Venice* there are only two scenes not ending so (II. iii and vii), and in the second of these Portia's withdrawal is implied. It follows that "dead" bodies always had to be carried off the stage in the action of the play.

It was not unknown for the stage floor to be equipped with a trap-door for the sudden appearance and disappearance of ghosts and spirits, and some theatres had a flying apparatus by which such could descend on the stage with the aid of ropes on runners. Under the stage was an orchestra, a very important feature of the Elizabethan theatre. It was used in the last scene of *The Merchant of Venice*, a moonlight scene of harmony after conflict, the happiest scene in all Shakespeare, as well as for music while Bassanio commented on the caskets and for one or two flourishes of cornets.

At the back of the stage was a recess ("within"), and this was curtained and could be shut off when desired. The caskets would, no doubt, be "within", while Portia and the various attendants would hold the main stage. Indeed, at the beginning of Act II, Sc. vii, Portia says, "Go *draw aside the curtains*, and discover the several caskets to this noble prince." This is repeated when Arragon chooses, and in III. ii we have the stage direction, "Curtain drawn from before the caskets".

Above the recess was a balcony, which served for castle walls, an upper room and suchlike scenes. This too could be curtained off. Judging from the way opportunities are made for balcony scenes in Elizabethan plays people were very fond of them, particularly when there was an escape from the balcony—an upper room, for example—to the main stage—representing the ground below. In Act II, Sc. vi we have the successive stage directions, "Enter Jessica, *above*, in boy's clothes", "Exit above", and

"Enter Jessica, *below*", and before coming down Jessica throws a casket to Lorenzo, who is on the main stage below.

People who wanted to be in the public eye were able to hire stools actually on the stage itself. Payment of one shilling extra entitled them to have their pipes lit by a page, thus showing to all and sundry that they were in a position to be attended. Such a privilege would be valued by country gentlemen who wanted it to be known that they had come up to town. It was a source of continual annoyance to playwrights that actors "gagged" in order to please these aristocratic playgoers.

No women were allowed to act by law. Consequently women's parts were taken by boys with unbroken voices. Imagine a boy's rendering of Lady Macbeth! This accounts for the few women's parts in plays of the period, though some were always introduced for the sake of variety. It also accounts for the large number of plays where a woman disguises herself as a page boy. It made it much easier for the producer; further, the audience was intrigued by a situation in which a character was pretending to be what he really was! In *The Merchant of Venice* every one of the female characters takes on male disguise.

Plays were not acted in period costume, though frequently *some* attempt was made to suggest a period, and the result must often have been a bizarre compromise. Thus all Shakespeare's plays can be said to have been first acted in "modern dress". Although there was no scenery, managers spared no expense on the most lavish of costumes.

On days when the theatre was open a flag was flown from the turret, and when the play was about to begin a trumpet was sounded. The turret of the Globe Theatre, the best remembered of all the early theatres, housed a big alarum bell, a favourite theatrical effect.

Teachers will find Brodie's Filmstrip, *The Theatre in Shakespeare's Day*, helpful in presenting the theatre of *The Merchant of Venice* more vividly.

One must not imagine that it was difficult for Shakespeare to write plays for such a theatre. It would have been difficult for him to write for any other than the one to which he was accustomed. What we have never known we can never miss.

THE TEXT OF SHAKESPEARE'S PLAYS

FEW readers of Shakespeare realise the difficulties that scholars have had to overcome in order to establish accurate texts of the plays. The First Folio (see p. 6), contained thirty-six plays. This is the basis of all subsequent editions. Other large-size collected editions, or Folios, were published in the seventeenth century, the Third and Fourth Folios containing seven additional plays, none of which, with the exception of *Pericles*, is now thought to be by Shakespeare. Sixteen of the plays had already been published separately as Quartos (editions half folio size) before 1623, and in the case of some plays, including *The Merchant of Venice*, more than one Quarto edition exists. Some of these Quartos, for example, those of *The Merchant of Venice*, are almost word for word the same as the texts in the First Folio and were possibly set up from Shakespeare's own manuscript or at least from accurate theatre copies; but others are shortened, inferior versions, possibly "pirated" editions published by some unauthorised person who had access to theatre copies or parts of them, or who had taken down the plays in short-hand while they were being performed. It is thought that the texts of the First Folio were set up from the good Quartos and from good theatre copies. But these texts must all be compared, printers' mistakes and other inter-ference traced, before a reliable text can be arrived at. The first editor to attempt the problem of the text was Nicholas Rowe (1674-1718), who also divided most of the plays into acts and scenes, supplied place-names of the location of each scene, indications of entrances and exits and a list of dramatis personæ, which are absent from many of the texts in the Quarto and Folio editions. In *The Merchant of Venice*, however, all the acts but no scenes are marked in the First Folio, all entrances and exits correspond with those of modern editions within a few lines (the greatest variation being a mere eight lines) and the text is practically the same as that recognised now. Rowe's scene-divisions are con-venient for reference (like the division of the books of the Bible into chapters and verses) but have no important use in Shakespearian study. They were fitted for the stage of

Rowe's time, but would have been to no purpose upon Shakespeare's stage with the barest of scenery.

While knowledge of the text is important for examination study, and, indeed, intelligent textual study can throw much light on an author, it should never be forgotten that the literary and dramatic aspects of the play are more vital. At the same time, study of the text is the basis of all literary and dramatic study.

TEXTUAL NOTES

ACT I. SCENE I

ANTONIO, who seems to have something on his mind, tells his friend Bassanio that he can count on him to provide the funds to fit Bassanio out in style to court Portia, a rich heiress, notwithstanding the fact that at the moment his assets are invested in cargoes now at sea and he cannot lay his hands on ready money.

At the outset the very first line of the play strikes the key-note of the whole. There seems to be a nameless dread hanging over Antonio, and the suspense of the audience is aroused.

Three of the four strands of the plot are set going in this, the first scene.

1. The Bond-plot, in which Shylock gets Antonio in his grip.

2. The Casket-plot, in which Bassanio wins Portia.

3. The Lorenzo-Jessica plot, in which Lorenzo elopes with Shylock's daughter (ll. 70-1).

In sooth. Note the natural way in which the play opens, as if Antonio is answering a question. We get the impression that the conversation to which we are now listening has been going on for some time.

sad, serious.

I am, I have yet.

want-wit, dullard, simpleton.

ado, difficulty.

argosies, large richly-laden merchant-ships.

signiors, gentlemen, noblemen. "Signor" is the Italian for "sir" or "Mr."

burghers, citizens.

flood, sea.

pageants, shows, displays. Shakespeare had no doubt seen such on the Thames.

overpeer, overlook.

traffickers, trading vessels.

curt'sy to them. The lighter ships, tossing on the waves, seem to be bowing to the steadier argosies.

woven wings, *i.e.* sails.

venture, commercial speculation. In Elizabethan times importing merchants were called "Merchant venturers".

forth, out.

The better . . . hopes, I should always be thinking of the ships on which my hopes depended. "Affections" = feelings.

still, always—the usual meaning in Elizabethan English.

plucking . . . wind, *i.e.* plucking a blade of grass to hold up to tell the direction of the wind, or perhaps plucking a handful of grass to throw up into the air for the same purpose.

Peering in, poring over.

roads, roadsteads, where a ship may *ride* at anchor. *Cf.* Yarmouth *roads.*

out of doubt, doubtless.

flats, sandbanks.

Andrew. Suggested as the name of a ship.

dock'd, embedded.

Vailing . . . burial, lowering her top-sail beneath her hull so as to touch the sand which buried her.

straight, straightway.

touching but, merely touching.

this. Accompanied by some gesture indicating great value, *e.g.* the arms stretched out wide.

now, the next moment.

Shall I . . . sad? If I can imagine all these things, how can I be without the thought that if they really happened it would make me grave? Notice Salarino's illustrations. (1) His breath on his soup would remind him of winds on the sea. (2) The sand in the hour-glass would remind him of sandbanks. (3) The stone church would remind him of dangerous rocks.

to think upon, from thinking about.

bottom, ship. (Synecdoche—the part uppermost in the mind for the moment, the hold storing the cargo.)

estate, property, fortune. Still the legal term for the property of which a person dies possessed.

Upon, dependent upon.

fortune, chance.

Not . . . neither. In Elizabethan English a double negative intensifies the idea, instead of logically cancelling it.

Janus. Roman god of gates and doors, represented with two heads, as a gate faces two ways. (One head was that of an old man and one that of a young man, symbolising the past and the future.) The point of Salarino's oath is that in the dispositions of men there are similarly opposite extremes. The festival of Janus was at the turn of the year (*i.e.* our year), when the sun began to grow stronger, the day dividing the past from the future (whence *Janu*ary).

peep through their eyes, *i.e.* laugh so much that their faces are screwed up.

like parrots, *i.e.* without any understanding, or perhaps it simply means with a screech like a parrot's.

at a bag-piper, *i.e.* even at melancholy music.

vinegar, *i.e.* sour.

Nestor. An old and wise Greek. If *he* laughed it *must* have been a good joke!

comes. Really "come", but the verb is no doubt attracted to "Bassanio", the noun next to it. This is common in Elizabethan English. Further, Bassanio is the most important of the three.

prevented, forestalled. The literal meaning of the word—"pre" = before, and "venire" (Lat.) = to come. *Cf.* the Prayer Book, "Prevent us, O Lord, in all our doings".

embrace the occasion, take the opportunity.

when shall we laugh? when shall we have a good time together?

strange, *i.e.* a stranger to me—I haven't seen you for a long time.

must it be so? must you go? Bassanio senses that Salarino and Salanio are leaving because of his arrival.

We'll make . . . yours, whenever you care to fix up an appointment we'll make it convenient. Bassanio later fixes up a supper party (II. ii).

where we must meet. Later on we see that Lorenzo and Jessica have planned an elopement.

You look not well. The fact that different people independently notice the change in Antonio impresses it upon us.

respect upon, care about. The line could be rendered, "You take life too seriously".

They lose . . . care, if a man buys the whole world he has nothing for his pains if the worry of it pulls him down. "Care" = worry, anxiety.

as the world, *i.e.* for what it is worth.

play the fool, *i.e.* in life's play—continuing Antonio's metaphor of the previous line.

With mirth and laughter. *Not* owing to "sadness".

liver. Thought of by the Elizabethans as the seat of the affections.

mortifying, causing death.

his grandsire, *i.e.* an effigy of his grandsire.

mantle. The stagnant pond looks as if it has a garment cast over it. "Cream" and "mantle" are nouns used as verbs—in Elizabethan English any part of speech was commonly used as another.

a wilful stillness entertain, keep up an obstinate silence.

With purpose . . . opinion of, on purpose to get a reputation for.

conceit, power of thought.

who, he who, one who.

Sir Oracle. As if speaking with the authority of a god.

therefore only, for that reason alone (that they say nothing).

almost damn . . . fools, would almost damn those who heard them, because they would have to call them fools. They would be damned for calling their brothers fools according to *Matthew*, v. 22.

melancholy bait, bait of melancholy.

fool gudgeon. Implying that the gudgeon is very easy to catch and worthless when it is caught.

for this gear, on account of what you say.

Is that anything. Is there any sense in that?

speaks an infinite deal of nothing, talks a great deal of nonsense.

disabled, impaired, so that it is *unable* to bear my expenses.

something, somewhat, to some extent.

showing . . . continuance, living above my income. "Of" is required after "continuance" to complete the sense. "Port" = style, *cf.* de*port*ment.

make moan . . . rate, complain at having such a lordly expenditure cut down.

fairly, honourably.

gaged, pledged.

from your love I have a warranty, on account of your love for me I have a right.

stand within the eye of honour, be honourable. "Eye" = field of vision.

occasions, requirements. Whatever Bassanio requires that Antonio can supply is at his disposal.

shaft, arrow.

his fellow of the self-same flight, another arrow made to the same pattern (*i.e.* of the same length, and feathered and weighted the same, and therefore likely to fly in an identical way). "His" = its. "His" was the old neuter possessive as well as the masculine.

advised, careful.

childhood proof, illustration from childhood.

pure innocence, *i.e.* there is no trick in what I propose. I use this illustration from childhood because what follows is innocent (as childhood).

self, same.

or . . . or, either . . . or.

latter hazard, *i.e.* the second loan he is now asking for.

wind . . . circumstance, beat about the bush. The metaphor is from a sportsman stalking his game.

making . . . uttermost, doubting that I shall do the utmost I can for you.

prest unto, ready for.

that word, *i.e.* the word "fair".

sometimes, formerly, on a previous occasion. *Cf.* a *sometime* scholar.

undervalued, inferior.

Brutus' Portia. Portia, wife of Brutus, chief of the murderers of Julius Cæsar. Both are characters in Shakespeare's play *Julius Cæsar*.

Colchos. Jasons. Colchis was a land at the eastern end of the Black Sea. Æetes, the king, had a golden fleece, to obtain which he had murdered one of Jason's relatives. Pelias, Jason's uncle, had usurped his throne, but promised to give Jason back his kingdom if he captured the golden fleece, which was guarded by a dragon. Jason set out at the head of the Argonauts (sailing in the ship *Argo*), and ultimately was successful through the help of Medea, daughter of the King of Colchis. Medea then fled with Jason and became his wife.

rival place, place as a rival.

presages, which presages. Shakespeare often omits the relative pronoun.

thrift, success.

Thou know'st . . . sea. Antonio had not admitted so much to Salarino (ll. 42-4).

commodity, property (on which to raise a loan—a "present (*i.e.* immediate) sum").

presently, immediately (the literal meaning). See note on "commodity", above.

no question make, have no doubt.

of my trust or for my sake, on credit (as a business deal) or for my own sake personally (as a friend).

Act I. Scene ii

A scene in a play may do one or more of the following:

1. Give the exposition (usually in the early part of the play).

2. Advance the action.

3. Create an atmosphere.

4. Develop a character.

5. Give dramatic relief—contrast.

6. Make an impression of the flight of time between two other scenes.

This scene is expository—a scene of explanation for the benefit of the audience, so that the audience will understand what follows. Portia and her maid Nerissa talk of the casket-lottery, a stipulation of her dead father's will that her husband must be the suitor who chooses a certain one of three caskets. Her wooers are passed in review, ending up with Bassanio, who is obviously the only one in whom she is at all interested. The scene ends with the announcement of another suitor, the Prince of Morocco.

Portia's lively wit is a happy contrast to the "sadness" of Antonio and Bassanio in Scene i (although, to begin with, she, too, is feeling "sad"). Contrast is a fundamental principle in Shakespeare's dramatic art.

this great world. Her suitors came from all over Europe, and from Morocco as well.

mean happiness, small happiness.

with mean, between the two (misery and good fortune).

superfluity, people who have too much. Abstract for concrete, as frequently in Elizabethan English.

comes by, gets.

competency, people who have enough without excess. Another abstract term, contrasted with "superfluity".

sentences, maxims.

chapels had been churches, small churches would have been large ones. (Nothing to do with Nonconformist chapels.)

easier, more easily—adjective for adverb (see note on "mantle", p. 40).

blood, passions.

in the fashion to choose, much help in choosing.

by the will. A pun on the word, here meaning last will and testament.

nor . . . none. See note on "Not . . . neither", p. 39.

who chooses . . . you, he who chooses the one which he intended shall fulfil the condition and become your husband. This and what follows is naturally introduced into the conversation for the benefit of the audience. For "who" see note p. 40.

thee. thou. "Thou" was a sign of familiarity—the usual address from masters to servants or between close companions: "you" was a more formal form of address. Notice how Nerissa addresses Portia by the more formal "you".

over-name them, name them over, go over them.

level, guess, *lit.* "aim"—a metaphor from levelling a weapon to take aim—"have a shot at", as we say.

colt. With a pun on its slang meaning—a rough fellow. The Neapolitans were famous for their horsemanship.

appropriation, addition.

parts, qualities.

County Palatine, Count of the Palatinate, a state on the upper Rhine. Further on Portia calls him "the *Count* Palatine".

An, if.

choose, *i.e.* somebody else, as much as to say, "You don't know what you're missing".

the weeping philosopher. Heraclitus, Greek philosopher of Ephesus, sixth century, B.C.

sadness. See note on "sad", p. 38.

death's head . . . mouth, *i.e.* skull and cross-bones.

by, about.

he hath . . . Neapolitan's, *i.e.* according to him.

better, more exaggerated.

every man in no man, he has no personality, he suits himself to his company, as we say—in Rome he does as Rome does.

twenty husbands. Because he is "every man in no man".

What say you to, what do you think of? Portia purposely misunderstands Nerissa.

come into the court, bear me witness.

proper man's picture, picture of a handsome man.

suited, dressed.

doublet, tunic.

round hose, short, puffed-out breeches. The Englishman's mixing up of foreign fashions to show that he had travelled in various countries is a stock subject of Elizabethan satire. Nowadays he leaves the labels on his suit-case or "G.B." on his car!

charity, love (as in *I Corinthians*, xiii).

borrowed, received.

became his surety, *i.e.* to see that the debt was repaid.

sealed under for another, signed his name (and put his "seal") under the Scot's on a document stating that the Scot's debt would be repaid (*i.e.* by "another" box on the ear). This is a hit at the frequent alliances between the Scots and the French which caused England constant embarrassment, as she was liable to be attacked on two fronts.

An the worst . . . fell, *i.e.* if nobody wants me for a wife. "Fall" = happen, *be*fall.

Rhenish wine, white or pale yellow wine, from the valley of the Rhine.

contrary, wrong. She is joking, of course, for obviously she has not told Nerissa which is the right casket.

is. Singular, because they have all determined on the same thing.

by some other sort, in some other way.

imposition, conditions *imposed.*

Sibylla. Strictly speaking, not a proper name. There were several Sibyls, or prophetesses. Shakespeare is no doubt thinking of the one who was granted by Apollo to live as many years as she could hold grains of sand in her hand.

Diana. Roman goddess of the moon and of hunting, represented as a virgin goddess.

are. See note on "comes", p. 39.

in your father's time. This was the "sometimes" referred to by Bassanio, I. i. 163.

as I think, so was he called. Added to cover up her obvious delight in Bassanio, as much as to say, "I can't quite remember his name".

four strangers. Nerissa mentioned six. It has been suggested that four was the original number, but Shakespeare added the English and Scots lords to give an opportunity for topical "hits", and forgot to alter the number here. He was never very careful over details like this.

condition, disposition.

the complexion of a devil, *i.e.* black.

shrive me, hear my confession (because he has "the condition of a saint").

Sirrah, fellow.

Act I. Scene iii

Antonio, who has no love of Shylock, is forced to borrow money from him for the sake of his friend Bassanio. Shylock agrees to lend the money, and without interest, but suggests a "merry bond", under which the penalty of default will be a pound of Antonio's flesh.

At the end of Act I all the main characters have been introduced, and the situations which bring them together explained. Bassanio's final words leave us with a sense of foreboding for the future.

ducats. A ducat was worth about 4s. 6d. Multiply this by about twenty to get the value in modern money.

bound, become surety, as Portia says of the Frenchman in Sc. ii.

May you stead, can you help? For "stead" (and also "pleasure") see note on "mantle", p. 40.

pleasure, favour.

shall I know your answer? Bassanio wants Shylock to say yes or no. Shylock enjoys keeping waiting a Christian who is seeking a favour of him and postpones his decision.

Antonio is a good man. As Shylock explains in his next speech, he is referring to Antonio's substance—a deal with him would be a sound investment.

sufficient, *i.e.* as a surety.

are in supposition, exist only in theory.

argosy. See note p. 38.

Tripolis. A port in the Lebanon. (Not Tripoli in Libya.)

Rialto. Exchange.

ventures. See note p. 38.

squandered, scattered. What Antonio regards as good business—not having all his eggs in one basket (see Sc. i, ll. 42-4)—Shylock calls in question.

I will be assured. Shylock purposely misunderstood Bassanio, as if he had meant, "Wait until you are sure". This gives him longer to gloat over the Christian's necessity.

habitation . . . into, *i.e.* flesh of the pig, referring to the time when Christ cast devils into swine. See *Matthew*, viii. 28-34. "Nazarite" = Nazarene, an inhabitant of Nazareth. "Nazarite" was the word used in all translations of the Bible before the Authorised Version of 1611. Now there is a distinction between the two words and a "Nazarite" means a Hebrew who had taken certain vows of abstinence.

publican, tax-collector. *Cf. Luke*, xviii. 10-13.

for, because. "For that", in the next line, has the same meaning.

simplicity, foolishness. *Cf.* when we say somebody is "simple", or a "simpleton".

usance, interest (for the *use* of money).

catch . . . hip, catch hold of him by the hips, and so throw him and get the better of him. A metaphor from wrestling.

where . . . congregate, *i.e.* the Rialto. Antonio attacks him even in the midst of the business world (where his chances of profit are greatest).

thrift, profit, gain.

debating of, considering.

near, approximate, *i.e.* he cannot work it out exactly without seeing his accounts.

gross, full amount.

Tubal. A name occurring in *Genesis*, x. 2.

soft! A common exclamation of the time, equivalent to, "Wait a minute!"

Rest you fair. A contraction of the salutation "God rest (*i.e.* keep) you fair"—an ingenious way of getting round a law which forbade the profane use of the name of God on the stage.

in our mouths, *i.e.* about whom we were speaking.

lend . . . giving. "Taking" refers to "lend", and "giving" to "borrow".

excess, interest, an amount in *excess* of the principal.

ripe, urgent. Metaphor from ripe fruit needing to be plucked at once.

possessed, informed of.

would, would have, want.

I had forgot. Shylock is here trying to disguise the eagerness he had involuntarily shown in answering Antonio's question to Bassanio.

you told me so. Spoken to Bassanio.

Methought, *lit.* it seemed to me. "Thought" is an impersonal verb, and "me" is in the dative case.

Upon advantage, with interest, or "excess".

I do never use it, it is never my custom.

When Jacob . . . sheep. See *Genesis*, xxx. 25-43.

his wise mother. Rebecca. See *Genesis*, xxvii. 31-40.

third possessor. Third *including* Abraham as the first. We should say *second from* Abraham.

were compromised, had made an agreement together.

eanlings, new-born lambs.

pied, irregularly marked, spotted, "party-coloured".

pilled me, pealed. The "me" (ethic dative) has no meaning. It simply stands for the person indirectly interested in the fact stated.

eanlings, lambs.

blest, fortunate.

served for, *i.e.* as his "hire". Antonio implies that the usurer does no service for his return.

Was this . . . good? did you mention this to justify interest? That may have been Shylock's purpose in introducing the story of Jacob and Laban, or it may have been simply to gain time while he was thinking out his plan of revenge.

falsehood, deceit.

beholding, beholden.

Still. See note p. 39.

sufferance, endurance, patience.

badge, *i.e.* special characteristic.

for use of, because I use. *Cf.* note on "for", p. 45.

Go to, consider. We say, "Come".

void your rheum, spit.

your suit, what you seek (*sue* for).

bondman's key, tones of a slave.

bated, lessened, here "whispering".

breed, *i.e.* interest.

Who . . . penalty. Notice the change in the construction of this sentence. The subject was going to be "who" ("thine enemy"), but Antonio changes it to "thou", thus bringing home his argument more directly to Shylock. This shows his strong feeling ("storming"). Certainly it cannot be said here that Antonio is "fawning". "Break" = break his agreement, fail to repay at the appointed time.

doit, farthing (a Dutch coin).

kind, kindness.

were, would be (subjunctive mood). Bassanio can hardly believe his ears.

notary, law-officer who draws up or attests (*notes*) deeds, etc.

your single bond, a bond signed by you alone, *i.e.* without any other security. Shylock wishes to make the agreement seem as informal as possible. Really he wishes to prevent anyone else paying the debt as surety for Antonio, should he default.

condition, agreement.

nominated for, assessed at.

equal, exact.

Content, I am content. An exclamation of acceptance.

break. See note on "Who . . . penalty", above.

not . . . neither. See note p. 39.

muttons, beef. Words of French derivation (moutons, bœufs) for sheep and oxen. Now the Old English words are used for the living animal and those of French derivation for the dead flesh only.

extend, offer.

so, let it be so, well and good.

fearful, risky, insecure, causing *me* fear.

unthrifty knave, wastrel, good-for-nothing fellow—Launcelot Gobbo.

presently. See note p. 41.

dismay, cause for us to be dismayed.

REVISION QUESTIONS ON ACT I

1. How do Antonio's friends account for his sadness? How do *you* account for it?

2. Enumerate Portia's suitors and give her opinion of any two of them, pointing out anything witty in her description of them.

3. What impression have you of Bassanio's character from this Act alone?

4. Describe the first meeting in the play between Antonio and Shylock.

5. What are the reasons for Shylock's violent hatred of Antonio? How far do you think he had cause for hating Antonio?

ACT II. SCENE I

The Prince of Morocco, whose arrival at Portia's house was announced at the end of Act I, Sc. ii, decides to venture to win Portia by trying his fortune in the casket-lottery.

The large number of short scenes in Act II gives an impression that much is happening, and at the beginning of Act III we can readily believe that three months have passed. No words can give a sense of the flight of time in the same way as the actual passing of events before the eyes of the audience.

shadow'd . . . sun, dark-coloured garment given by the glowing sun. In Elizabethan English a livery was any kind of dress.

To whom . . . bred, *i.e.* Morocco is near the equator.

fairest, *i.e.* in complexion, in the sense in which we use the word when we speak of "fair" hair.

Phœbus. Roman sun-god.

whose blood is reddest. Deep-red blood was supposed to be a sign of courage. Strictly speaking it should be "redder", but the superlative is often used in Elizabethan English where we should use the comparative.

fear'd, caused to fear.

best-regarded, thought most highly of.

clime, country.

steal your thoughts, win your affection.

In terms, with regard to the conditions.

nice, finicking.

scanted, restricted.

hedged, bound (as a hedge denies freedom).

wit, understanding. See note on "want-wit", p. 38.

that means I told you. A dramatic necessity that this information should be supposed to have been given to Morocco off the stage, as the audience have already learnt it from Act I, Sc. ii.

stood as fair, would have stood as good a chance. Portia, of course, means that she does not care much for any of them, but Morocco interprets it as an encouragement.

Sophy. Shah of Persia.

fields of, battles from.

Sultan Solyman. Solyman the Magnificent (1490-1566), Sultan of Turkey, 1520-66, defeated by the Persians, 1535.

alas the while! An intensified form of "alas".

Hercules and Lichas. Hercules was a Roman hero (Greek Heracles) of enormous strength, and Lichas his "page". Morocco means that in a game of chance the page Lichas might beat the hero Hercules, and so in the lottery of the caskets may he be beaten by an "unworthier" man.

which, to decide which.

Alcides. Hercules. The ending "-ides" means "son of". Actually Hercules was the grandson of Alcæus.

blind Fortune. Fortune was represented as blindfold, symbolical of the unaccountable and capricious variations in her dispensations to different men.

be advised, consider (before you take such an irrevocable step). *Cf.* note p. 41.

to the temple. In order to take the oath.

blest, most blest. The superlative in "cursed'st" is carried over into the antithetical "blest".

ACT II. SCENE II

Launcelot Gobbo leaves the service of Shylock for that of Bassanio. Gratiano gets Bassanio's consent to accompany him to Belmont.

will serve, probably "will *have* to serve".

fiend, *i.e.* devil.

with thy heels. As an animal kicks up its heels and makes off.

pack, be off. *Cf.* the phrase "to send someone *packing*".

Via! Away.

heavens, heavens' sake.

hanging . . . heart. So preventing his natural impulse ("heart") from having its own way.

did something smack, dishonourable, not above board.

grow to. A phrase used of milk burnt in a saucepan and so having an unpleasant taste.

God bless the mark! God forgive me (for mentioning the devil), "saving your reverence". "The mark" is probably the sign of the Cross.

saving your reverence, with all due respect to you.

incarnation. Launcelot's malapropism for "incarnate".

master Jew's. The fact that Gobbo does not think it necessary to name Shylock shows how well he is known.

sand-blind, half-blind.

high-gravel-blind. Launcelot's improvement on "sand-blind".

confusions. For "conclusions" (malapropism).

marry. An oath. *Lit.* "by the Virgin Mary", though not used with this signification. It corresponds simply to some such exclamation as "Indeed!"

sonties, saints.

dwell. This second time the word is used it obviously means "is there now".

Master. Emphasised, as a reproof to his father for omitting his title.

raise the waters, *i.e.* create a storm, stir things up.

well to live, of good life, or perhaps "well off"—emphasising Old Gobbo's lack of intelligence, since it contradicts what he has just said.

a', corruption of "he".

ergo, therefore (Lat.). Launcelot is showing off his knowledge.

mastership. Irony—Gobbo is willing to call the young man he has met in the street "master", but not his own son!

father. Dramatic irony. A common form of address to an old man, and Gobbo does not suspect that he is talking with his son.

Sisters Three. The three Fates in Greek mythology, one of whom held the spindle, while the second wove man's fate upon it, until the third cut the web (symbolising the end of a man's life).

you. Emphasised, as much as to say, "*You* won't understand my references to the Fates and Destinies and Sisters Three".

hovel-post, the post supporting the roof of a hovel.

God rest. See note on "Rest you fair", p. 45. Here the name of God has been allowed to stand.

thou. See note on "thee. thou", p. 43. Gobbo changes from the formal "you" as soon as he realises that it is Launcelot to whom he is speaking.

Lord worshipped, would to God.

fill-horse, shaft-horse. The "fills" or "thills" were the shafts of a cart. Launcelot kneels with his *back* to his father, and so his father feels the back of his head instead of his face and imagines him to have grown a beard.

set up my rest, made up my mind. A term from an Elizabethan card-game.

run some, run over some.

tell, count. This sentence is, of course, a humorous inversion of Launcelot's real meaning.

give me. See note on "pilled me", p. 46.

gives rare new liveries. Bassanio's preparation to go to Belmont were evidently "town talk".

to, go to. The verb of motion was often omitted.

anon, at once (*lit.* in one).

Gramercy, many thanks (Fr. "grand merci").

specify, certify (malapropism). So also "frutify", below. Similarly "infection" for "affection", "impertinent" for "pertinent", "defect" for "effect".

cater-cousins, good friends.

preferr'd, recommended. See Shylock's last speech in Act I, Sc. iii, and Act II, Sc. v, ll. 49-51.

old proverb. "The grace of God is wealth enough."

parted, divided.

guarded, trimmed with braid.

I cannot get a service . . . head. This is perhaps what Shylock had told Launcelot, and now he repeats it in triumph.

table, tablet (referring to his palm, on which is written his future fortunes).

swear upon a book. This is not a connected sentence. Probably the sight of his open palm reminds Launcelot of a witness in a court of law placing his hand on the Bible to take the oath.

coming-in, allowance.

for this gear. See note p. 40.

orderly bestow'd, arranged in order.

suit to, request to make of, favour to ask of.

deny, refuse, forbid.

thee. After addressing Gratiano as "you", Bassanio changes to "thee" in adopting a friendly, persuasive tone.

Parts, qualities.

liberal, free and easy.

allay, temper.

modesty, moderation.

misconstrued, misjudged.

habit, demeanour, behaviour.

with respect, carefully, seriously. See note on "respect upon", p. 40.

demurely, gravely.

hood, cover.

Thus with my hat. It was the custom for hats to be worn at official dinners.

civility, good manners.

ostent, appearance, demonstration.

bearing, behaviour, "habit".

gauge, judge.

suit of mirth. Here a metaphor from a suit of clothes.

Act II. Scene iii

As Launcelot leaves Shylock's house Jessica gives him a letter to take to Lorenzo, who is a guest at the house of Launcelot's new master, Bassanio.

some taste, a little.

there is a ducat for thee. Jessica's generosity contrasts with her father's meanness.

exhibit, inhibit, or perhaps prohibit, stop. (Malapropism.)

though . . . manners, though I am his daughter by birth, I have not inherited his character.

strife, *i.e.* her divided loyalty, to her father and to her husband-to-be.

ACT II. SCENE IV

Jessica's letter is delivered to Lorenzo. It contains a plan for their elopement.

in, at.

Disguise. For the masque (see l. 22). This is to be at Bassanio's farewell party, to which he referred at the end of Sc. ii.

spoke, bespoken.

quaintly order'd, gracefully or artistically arranged.

in my mind. We now say "*to* my mind".

undertook. Like "spoke" a past participle.

furnish us, get ready.

Friend Launcelot, what's the news? Evidently this was not the first time that Launcelot had carried messages between Jessica and Lorenzo.

break up, open. A natural term to use of opening a letter sealed with wax.

the hand, the handwriting. Later punning on the usual sense.

prepare you, prepare yourselves. *Cf.* the reflexive use of "us" in ll. 2, 4 and 8.

masque. A torchlight procession, in which those who took part wore masks.

straight. See note p. 39.

she do it, *i.e.* misfortune do it. The next "she" refers to Jessica.

faithless, unbelieving.

ACT II. SCENE V

Shylock gives Jessica directions concerning the care of his house before he leaves to go to supper at Bassanio's.

Notice the dramatic irony of this, for all the time the audience knows of Jessica's plot to elope with Lorenzo; also the suspense in Shylock's waverings whether to go or not, and Shylock's uneasy sense of presentiment.

without bidding, *i.e.* on my own initiative.

bid forth, asked out.

to-night, last night.

reproach, approach (malapropism). Shylock's reply concerns the actual word Launcelot used—he will expect Bassanio's reproach if his plot against Antonio succeeds.

And they have conspired together. Notice the dramatic irony in this remark. Launcelot means the supper party, *we* think of Lorenzo and Jessica.

masque. See note p. 51.

Black-Monday. Easter Monday, originally the Easter Monday of 1360 (14th April), so called because it was such a bitterly cold day that many soldiers of King Edward III, then besieging Paris, died on their horses' backs from cold. Launcelot, of course, is making fun of Shylock's words, "For I did dream of money-bags to-night".

four year, four years ago.

wry-neck'd fife, curved flute; or perhaps the player, who turns his neck round as he plays.

varnish'd. Because wearing masks.

forth. See note on "bid forth", p. 51.

to-night, this coming night, not as p. 51.

Hagar's offspring, a Gentile—the off-spring of Abraham by his bond-woman Hagar.

patch, fool, referring to the motley (patched) dress of the professional fool.

profit, profitable work.

crost, interfered with.

Act II. Scene vi

Lorenzo calls for Jessica, who elopes with him disguised in boy's clothes, bringing some of her father's treasure with her.

pent-house, that part of a house projecting over the street, as houses commonly did in Elizabethan times.

out-dwells, out-stays.

pigeons. Actually it was doves which drew the chariot of Venus, Roman goddess of love, and were sacred to her.

To keep obliged faith unforfeited, to keep faith that has been pledged ("obliged") unbroken.

That ever holds, that is always the case.

untread again his measures, retrace his steps.

unbated. See note on "bated", p. 46.

All things . . . enjoy'd. We might paraphrase, "To travel hopefully is better than to arrive".

younker, youngster—and therefore smart.

prodigal. The parable of the Prodigal Son (*Luke*, xv. 11-32) was evidently in Shakespeare's mind.

scarfed, decorated with flags and streamers.

puts from, sets out from.

over-weather'd, weather-beaten to excess.

ribs. See note on "Vailing . . . burial", p. 39.

above, in boy's clothes. See p. 33.

who. Strictly speaking should be "whom".

thy thoughts, *i.e.* in your heart of hearts you surely know that I love you.

exchange, *i.e.* change into boy's clothes.
Cupid. Roman god of love.
my torch-bearer. *Cf.* what Lorenzo says in Sc. iv, l. 23.
light. Punning on "bright" and "frivolous".
an office of discovery, a job which will show things up.
obscured, hidden.
garnish, dress.
But come at once. The short line gives emphasis.
close, hiding, concealing.
doth play the runaway, is fast slipping away.
stay'd, waited.
gild. Another pun—(1) provide with gold, (2) adorn.
hood, *i.e.* in which he is masked.
Gentile. A pun on "genteel".
Beshrew me, *lit.* "curse me", but in actual use not any stronger than "bother" or even "indeed".
but I, if I do not.
if that. *Cf.* note on "for", p. 45.
stay. See note above.
nine o'clock. In Sc. ii Bassanio said supper was to be ready "at the furthest by five of the clock", and in Sc. iv Lorenzo said the masque was fixed for six.
is come about, has changed round.
on't, of it.

ACT II. SCENE VII

The Prince of Morocco tries his luck at the caskets, chooses the golden one and thereby fails to win Portia.

discover, uncover.
several, separate, different.
who. "Who" and "which" were interchangeable in Elizabethan English. *Cf.* the Lord's Prayer, "Our Father, *which* art in heaven".
all, quite.
blunt. A pun, (1) not sharp, (2) pointless.
The one, *i.e.* the right one.
withal, in addition (to the picture).
back again, in the reverse order.
golden, *i.e.* first-rate.
shows, appearances.
virgin. The whiteness of the silver being a symbol of virgin purity.
even, impartial.
rated by thy estimation, valued according to your own estimate.
disabling. See note on "disabled", p. 40.
shrine, image.
mortal-breathing saint, saint alive and breathing—not just a sculptured image.
Hyrcanian. Hyrcania was a district south and south-east of the Caspian Sea.
head, *i.e.* the crests of the waves.

it were . . . grave, lead would be too common a metal to enclose ("rib"—as the ribs enclose the body) her shroud in the darkness of the grave (*i.e.* too common a metal even for her coffin).

immured, shut up, as between four walls (Lat. "murus", Fr. "mur" = wall).

undervalued. See note p. 41.

coin . . . angel. The "angel" was Michael, shown piercing the dragon, whence the coin got its name of an "angel". Its value was about ten shillings.

insculp'd upon, in relief, embossed on top of the coin (whereas the picture of *this* angel was *inside* the casket).

thrive I as I may! Be my success what it will.

carrion Death, fleshless skull, death's head.

Gilded tombs . . . infold, gilded tombs (no less than those of inferior metals) contain worms.

had not been inscroll'd, would not have been written on a scroll (but would have been the picture of Portia). For "had" = would have, see note on "chapels had been churches", p. 42.

part, depart.

complexion, nature—not the meaning in Sc. i, l. 1. (Portia is not making fun of his colour.)

Act II. Scene VIII

Salarino and Salanio talk of Shylock's rage when he discovered that his daughter had stolen his jewels and gone off with a Christian, and of Antonio's grief at parting from Bassanio even for a short time.

raised, roused.

certified, informed.

passion, outburst of strong feeling.

day, *i.e.* the day upon which his bond becomes due for payment. Since Jessica has eloped with a Christian, Shylock will be all the more likely, says Salanio, to take it out of Antonio, another Christian.

reason'd, talked.

the narrow seas. The usual name for the English Channel in Shakespeare's time.

miscarried, was wrecked.

fraught, freighted, laden.

were not, might not be.

You were best. The "you" is dative—*lit.* "it would be best for you".

Slubber, slur over hastily and carelessly.

the very riping of the time, as long as is necessary to make a success of it. Evidently Antonio does not know that Portia is to be won only by the casket lottery.

mind of love, loving mind.

ostents. See note p. 50.

conveniently, suitably.

there, at the point.

affection. See note on "The better . . . my hopes", p. 38.

sensible, sensitive.

he only . . . him, his only pleasure in life is in Bassanio's friendship.

quicken his embraced heaviness, enliven the depression which he clings to.

ACT II. SCENE IX

The Prince of Arragon tries his luck at the caskets and, choosing the silver one, he too fails in his quest.

his oath. See ll. 9-16.

election, choice.

never in . . . marriage. See Sc. i. ll. 39-42.

Lastly. Notice the emphasis given this word as the only word of the line.

so have I address'd me, for this have I prepared myself.

By, to apply to.

fond, foolish.

martlet, house-martin.

in the force and road of casualty, where accidents are more likely to happen to its nest.

jump, agree.

go about to cozen, try to cheat.

degrees, titles.

derived, obtained.

clear, unstained.

purchased. The use of this word implies that too often "honours" are purchased by money.

cover, cover their heads—keep their hats on in the presence of those of lower rank.

How much low . . . honour! how many who are really low as peasants in character would be picked out from possessors of honours to be put back where they rightly belong!

how much honour . . . new-varnish'd! how many really honourable in character would be picked from among poor people ("ruin" = refuse) to be set up again in honour!

schedule, scroll.

To offend . . . offices, no man can be prisoner and judge at the same time. Having failed, Arragon is condemning the terms which he agreed to abide by.

shadows kiss, fall in love with their own vain illusions, build castles in the air.

I wis, certainly.

sped, finished with.

By, in proportion to.

deliberate, those who choose with deliberation, who take a long time to make up their minds.

They have . . . lose, *i.e.* they are *too* clever; for all their intelligence ("wit") they cannot succeed. And from Portia's point of view they are wise, for she does not want them for husbands.

my lord. Portia's playful rejoinder to the servant's "my lady" shows on what good terms she is with her servants.

sensible regreets, tangible greetings, those which the *senses* can appreciate, not merely "commends and courteous breath" but "gifts of rich value". "*Regreets*" suggests that this is not the first time Bassanio has been to Belmont (see his last speech in Act I, Sc. i, and Nerissa's last speech but one in Act I, Sc. ii).

commends, compliments, salutations.

breath, words.

Yet, as yet.

likely, promising.

costly, rich.

fore-spurrer, messenger riding on in advance, harbinger.

anon. See note p. 50.

high-day, holiday, *i.e.* as if decked out for a festival. *Cf.* the phrase "high-days and holidays".

Cupid. See note p. 53.

post, messenger. So called because messengers obtained fresh relays of horses at "posts" (stationed at regular intervals) on the road.

Bassanio . . . be! O lord Love (*i.e.* Cupid) may it be Bassanio if it be thy will!

REVISION QUESTIONS ON ACT II

1. Describe (*a*) Bassanio's interview with Launcelot, or (*b*) Antonio's parting from Bassanio (as told by Salarino).

2. What were the inscriptions on the golden and silver caskets, and their contents? Compare and contrast the characters of the two princes who choose them.

3. What light is thrown in this Act upon the home-life of Shylock? Does Jessica appear to you to be a good daughter?

4. Briefly describe the part played by Launcelot in this Act.

5. Give a short account of the elopement of Jessica.

ACT III.   SCENE I

Reliable reports tell of Antonio's losses at sea, and Shylock, maddened by his daughter's flight with a Christian, swears to claim his bond. Tubal, who has been sent to find Jessica, brings further distress with the news of Jessica's wastefulness with Shylock's money although he has been unable to locate her, but also confirms the news of Antonio. He works on Shylock's feelings, alternately delighting him with news of Antonio's misfortunes and "torturing" him with news of Jessica's extravagance, playing with him as a cat plays with a mouse.

Notice the close connection between the Bond-plot and the Lorenzo-Jessica plot in this scene.

Rialto. See note p. 45.

yet. See note p. 56.

lives there unchecked, is rumoured without contradiction.

the narrow seas. See note p. 54.

Goodwins. The Goodwin Sands, off the Isle of Thanet, Kent.

I think they call the place. Such a casual touch emphasises more than any set local colour that the scene of the play is abroad.

flat, sandbank.

knapped, broke off, *i.e.* with her teeth.

crossing the plain highway, wandering from side to side (instead of keeping to the tale), or perhaps going by cross-roads instead of the main road.

Come, the full stop. In spite of Salanio's resolution to tell his tale "without any slips of prolixity", Salarino has to pull him up short.

say amen, give my blessing (*lit.* "say so let it be") to your prayer.

cross, interfere with, hinder.

the wings she flew withal, the disguise in which she made her escape.

complexion. See note p. 54.

dam. damned. Is it natural that Shylock should pun at such a moment? At times of great anxiety the mind seeks relief in a trivial occupation. We often read in the newspapers of men trapped and in great pain jesting with their rescuers.

the devil, *i.e.* Shylock. Notice how Shylock in his great emotion ignores Salarino's jests at his expense.

Rhenish. See note p. 43.

match, bargain.

used, accustomed.

smug, spruce and self-satisfied.

let him look to his bond. This repeated twice has a terrible insistence.

to lend . . . courtesy, *i.e.* without interest, for which Shylock said he hated him more than for being a Christian (I. iii).

it will feed my revenge. *Cf.* in Act I, Sc. iii,

> If I can catch him once upon the hip,
> I will feed fat the ancient grudge I bear him.

dimensions, limbs.

fed, is he not fed, etc.

sufferance. See note p. 46.

it shall go . . . instruction, the obstacles will have to be great if I fail to improve upon your example.

Frankfort. A German town famous for its fairs.

The curse. See *Deuteronomy*, xxviii. 15-68, and *Daniel*, ix. 11.

thou loss upon loss, as we say, "Throwing good money after bad".

Tripolis. See note p. 45.

turquoise. A precious stone of a pale blue colour.

Leah. Obviously Shylock's dead wife.

undone, bankrupt, ruined.

fee me an officer, book an officer (to arrest Antonio in a fortnight, as soon as his bond becomes due), paying him in advance.

merchandise, profits (after the removal of a competitor who lends money without interest).

ACT III. SCENE II

Bassanio wins Portia in the casket-lottery, and we are made to feel their real regard for one another. Portia gives him a ring to plight their troth, a ring which he is enjoined never to part with, lest "it presage the ruin of your love". The fortunes of Gratiano and Nerissa have been linked with those of Bassanio and Portia, and they are to be married, too. But at the height of such great happiness comes disturbing news of Antonio's misfortunes on Bassanio's account (Lorenzo and Jessica accompanying the messenger), and immediately after the wedding ceremony Bassanio is to post away to Venice to see what he can do, with a promise from Portia of all the help it is in her power to give.

Notice how all four plots meet in this scene, the three already mentioned in I. i (p. 38), and, in addition, the rings episode has here its beginning.

in, by your.

is it not love. Portia will not admit that she loves Bassanio until after his choice. However, she will go so far as to say she does not hate him!

quality, manner.

hath no tongue, but thought, cannot speak her love, she can only keep it in her thoughts.

some month or two. The "day or two" of l. 1 has now become "some month or two".

am forsworn, should be guilty of breaking my oath. The very temptation shows how Portia loves Bassanio.

So, *i.e.* forsworn.

so, therefore.

Beshrew. See note on "Beshrew me", p. 53.

o'erlook'd, bewitched.

naughty, evil, wicked—a much stronger word then than now.

bars, obstacles. She is referring to her father's will, to which before other suitors she had willingly submitted.

though yours, not yours, though yours in love, not your wife.

prove it so, should it prove so (that through your choice of the caskets I am not to be your wife).

peize. eke. Both mean to lengthen out ("peize" = Fr. "peser", to weigh down). The idea is emphasised by Portia's saying the same thing three times in different words.

election. See note p. 55.

the rack. An instrument of torture—a wooden frame on which victims were gradually stretched. Portia suggests that torture was a common penalty for treason.

fear the enjoying, fear that I may not enjoy, fear *for* the enjoyment.

as treason, as between treason.

speak anything, *i.e.* in order to be released.

Had been the very sum, would have been the very utmost.

teach me answers. *E.g.* Portia's "confess and live" suggests Bassanio's "confess and love".

If you . . . me out. As Nerissa said in I. ii, "The lottery . . . will, no doubt, never be chosen by any rightly but one who shall rightly love."

swan-like end. Referring to the old belief that a swan sang once in its life—just before its death.

proper, exactly.

my eye . . . for him, *i.e.* it will make Portia weep.

flourish, *i.e.* of trumpets, when the king is crowned at the coronation ceremony.

dulcet, sweet (Lat. "dulcis").

in, at (as p. 51).

presence, dignity, noble bearing.

Alcides. Hercules, grandson of Alcæus (see note p. 48). Hesione, daughter of Laomedon, king of Troy, was to be sacrificed to appease a sea-monster and was fastened to a rock on the sea-shore, when Hercules offered to slay the monster and rescue her in return for certain horses (which, incidentally, he did not get, although he performed his mission). Bassanio goes "with much more love" than Hercules, for he saved Hesione not for love of her but for a reward of horses; Portia represents Hesione, who was to be sacrificed ("I stand for sacrifice"), and the servants the Trojan women ("Dardanian wives").

bleared. Through crying.

Live thou, if you live. Portia is still comparing herself to Hesione and Bassanio to Hercules. If Bassanio wins through it means her rescue.

fancy, shallow, not true love.

bred, begotten.

Or . . . or. See note p. 41.

dies . . . lies, *i.e.* lives only a short while—no longer than the eyes are pleased—it has no basis "in the heart or in the head".

So. Bassanio is referring to the theme of the song. In spite of Portia's unwillingness to be "forsworn", she gives Bassanio a pretty plain hint. Is it an accident also that the first three lines of the song rhyme with "lead"?

shows, appearances.

themselves, like the real things.

season'd, as seasoning smothers the taste of "tainted" food. This is the first of a number of illustrations of cases where "the outward shows" are "least themselves". Dramatically Bassanio's long speech increases the suspense by delaying the moment of his choice.

a gracious voice, *i.e.* eloquent counsel.

sober brow, serious-looking clergyman.

approve, justify.

simple, simple-minded. *Cf.* note on "simplicity", p. 45.

his. See note on "his fellow of the self-same flight", p. 41.

all. See note p. 53.

Mars. Roman god of war.

have livers white as milk, *i.e.* are cowards. The liver was then considered the seat of the affections. *Cf.* note on "whose blood is reddest", p. 47.

assume but valour's excrement, assume only the outward sign of valour, *i.e.* their beards. *Lit.* "excrement" = outgrowth.

redoubted, feared.

purchase by the weight, *i.e.* due to cosmetics.

lightest. A pun—(1) lightest in weight, (2) lightest in character, *i.e.* those who carry greatest weight of powder and paint are lightest in character. *Cf.* the pun on "light", note p. 53.

crisped, curled.

snaky, like the folds of a snake in appearance, but the idea of deceitfulness seems to be implied also.

golden. It does not strike one as very tactful of Bassanio to specify "golden" locks, since that was the colour of Portia's hair (see his last speech in Act I, Sc. i). "Golden" hair was very fashionable in Shakespeare's time, since the Queen had fair hair (really light ginger, called "golden" for compliment). She herself in her old age wore a false head of golden hair.

wanton, playful.

supposed fairness, beauty that is not genuine, *i.e.* a made-up face.

known. Qualifies "locks", not "fairness".

The skull . . . sepulchre, the false head of hair is the real hair of someone now dead. "In" = being in.

guiled, guileful, *i.e.* treacherous.

Indian, dark. See note on "golden", above.

Midas. In return for a kindness Bacchus, god of wine, allowed Midas, king of Phrygia, to ask him any favour he wished. He asked that whatever he touched might be turned into gold. This was granted, but when he found that even his food turned to gold, he implored the god to take back his gift.

Which rather threatenest. This is just what Morocco thought. See II.vii. 18.

doubtful thoughts, doubting anxieties. *Cf.* "Take therefore no *thought* for the morrow" (*Matthew*, vi. 34).

rash-embraced, felt without due cause—as when someone "crosses the bridge before they come to it". *Cf.* note on "quicken his embraced heaviness", p. 55.

allay, calm.

measure, moderation.

scant. See note on "scanted", p. 48.

counterfeit, portrait.

so near creation, so like her actual self.

Move these eyes? The portrait is so life-like that Bassanio can almost imagine that he can see the eyes moving.

riding on the balls of mine, moving with my eye-balls.

Should. This word bears the emphasis, *i.e.* it is fitting that it should sunder.

Faster, more firmly, as when we say, "Make it fast".

unfurnish'd, unprovided (with a fellow eye).

shadow, picture. Notice the antithesis between "substance" and "shadow".

underprizing, undervaluing.

Doth limp behind, comes short of.

The continent, that which contains.

Chance as fair, may you always be as lucky.

hold your fortune for, consider your fortune (not necessarily *good* fortune) here to be.

gentle, courteous—the same force as in "*gentle*man".

by note, as directed (by the scroll).

to give and to receive, *i.e.* to give a kiss and to receive the lady.

prize, competition (*for* a prize).

account, esteem.

livings, estates, property. *Cf.* a clergyman's *living*.

term in gross, sum up. "Account", "sum", "in gross" are all metaphors from book-keeping.

unpractised, inexperienced.

than this, than in the fact that "she is not yet so old but she may learn".

She, because she.

is not bred so dull, has not been brought up so foolishly.

but now . . . even now, but now, a moment or two ago (just now), even now, from this very moment. *Cf.* note on "now", p. 39.

vantage, vantage-ground, opportunity.

exclaim on, cry out against.

powers, faculties.

there doth appear. The construction is, "Such confusion as doth appear . . ."

every something . . . not express'd, every separate cry, blended together, becomes a wild inarticulate uproar, but one in which joy is predominant, expressed in the tone of the utterances though the words are indistinguishable.

wish none from me, wish none to be away from me, begrudge me none.

bargain, contract.

so, provided that.

intermission, delay.

pertains to me, is a part of (appertains to) my character.

stood, depended.

falls. See note on "An the worst . . . fell", p. 43.

my very roof, *i.e.* the very roof of my mouth.

promise last, promises are lasting, or perhaps referring to this particular promise.

Achieved, won.

so. See note above.

shall. There is no special emphasis on this word: modern English would simply say "will".

infidel, *i.e.* Jessica, who is a Jewess.

Salerio. Many editors consider that this is not a new character but that Salanio is meant, on the grounds that Shakespeare would not introduce a new character so late in the play. This is more than probable, and were Salerio a messenger who appeared only in this scene it is not likely that Shakespeare would give him a name, but simply say "Messenger", as, for instance, in the previous scene, "Enter a Servant". Further, Gratiano knows him well—"Your hand, Salerio".

the growth of my new interest here, the short time in which I have been in my new position here. Bassanio is wondering whether he is not rather presumptuous in giving his friends welcome to Portia's house.

past all saying nay, *i.e.* he would not take "No" as an answer.

Nor well, unless in mind. Salerio means that Antonio's health will depend on how his mind reacts to the calamity with which he is faced—how he "takes it".

his estate, how he is.

Jasons. See note on "Colchos. Jasons", p. 41.

you. Bears the emphasis—*you* and not Shylock.

shrewd, bad.

turn . . . man, change so much the temperament of any self-possessed man.

worse and worse! Portia evidently notices some further change in Bassanio.

Rating. Refers, of course, to "I".

How much I was a braggart. Because he was in debt, and so had *less than* nothing, as he goes on to explain.

state, position. *Cf.* "estate" above, and note p. 39.

engaged, pledged.

mere, absolute.

feed, supply.

as, like, being as.

Issuing, pouring out.

hit. Metaphor from shooting at a target.

Barbary. The Barbary states were on the Mediterranean coast of North Africa.

should. See note on "shall", p. 61.

discharge, discharge his debt to.

confound, ruin. *Cf.* the *Te Deum*, "Let me never be confounded", *i.e.* damned.

impeach, question (implying that the equal position of aliens before the law is really non-existent).

magnificoes, nobles.

port, im*port*ance. See note on "showing . . . continuance", p. 40.

persuaded, argued.

envious plea of, hateful or malicious demand for.

deny. See note p. 50.

best-conditioned. See note on "condition", p. 44.

unwearied, most unwearied. The superlative is carried over from "best".

any, in anyone.

For me, on my account, so far as I am concerned.

deface, cancel.

cheer, countenance. *Cf.* the phrase, "Good cheer".

dear bought, *i.e.* by Antonio's sacrifice, without which Bassanio would never have come to Belmont.

miscarried. See note p. 54. Here the perfect tense.

I. Strictly speaking should be "me", after the preposition "between".

your love, *i.e.* your love for *me* (Antonio does not mean Portia).

No rest . . . twain, I will not delay seeing you again by resting.

ACT III. SCENE III

The date of expiry of Shylock's bond has come, Antonio is under arrest, and Shylock is impervious to all entreaty.

This scene fills in the time-gap while Bassanio journeys from Belmont to Venice.

the fool . . . gratis. The chief cause of Shylock's hatred of Antonio. See his last speech in III. i, and his aside in I. iii.

Thou call'dst me dog. A charge Antonio never denied, *e.g.* in I. iii, "I am as like to call thee so again".

naughty. See note p. 58.

fond. See note p. 55.

I'll have my bond. Notice Shylock's insistence on this, ll. 4, 12, 13 and 17.

dull-eyed, short-sighted, or perhaps compassionate—dull-eyed in the sense that his eyes are dimmed with tears.

Christian. This word bears the emphasis.

It. Used sarcastically of Shylock, whom Salarino cannot think of as a *person*, with normal human feeling.

impenetrable, impervious to all kindly feeling.

kept with, lived amongst.

his forfeitures, penalties due to him.

grant . . . hold, allow this penalty to hold good (in law).

commodity, trading rights.

impeach. See note p. 62. Notice how Antonio uses practically the same phrase as Salerio, both probably quoting Shylock.

Since . . . nations. It would be a very serious matter to the city if foreigners felt that their legal agreements might not be upheld in Venetian courts (if they found that the Duke could arbitrarily interfere with the law in favour of a Venetian citizen), for they would transfer their trade elsewhere.

hardly, with difficulty.

ACT III. SCENE IV

Leaving her household in charge of Lorenzo and Jessica, Portia, under pretence of keeping a vow "to live in prayer and contemplation", decides to follow after Bassanio to Venice with a scheme of her own to help her husband's friend.

conceit, conception, idea. See note p. 40.

lover, friend—a common meaning of the word in Elizabethan English. *Cf.* "bosom lover", l. 17 (we still speak of a "bosom-friend").

Than . . . enforce you, than your customary kindness can make you.

converse, associate.

waste, spend.

bear an equal yoke. Metaphor from two oxen yoked together.

needs, of necessity. *Cf.* "must needs be", l. 18.

lineaments, features.

spirit, character.

purchasing . . . soul, redeeming him who resembles ("the semblance of") the man who is to me as my own soul (*i.e:* Bassanio).

state. See note p. 62.

husbandry and manage, stewardship and management.

husband, husband's.

imposition. See note p. 44.

people, *i.e.* household, servants.

Padua. The University of Padua was celebrated for its Chair of Law. Padua is eighteen miles from the "common ferry" to Venice.

with imagined speed, as quick as thought.

tranect, ferry-boat.

common, public. *Cf.* House of *Commons*, Book of *Common* Prayer.

convenient. See note on "conveniently", p. 54.

of us, *i.e.* of seeing us.

habit, dress. (Fr. "habit" = coat.)

we are accomplished with that, we have accomplishments which (*i.e.* those of men).

braver, finer. In Elizabethan English the word "brave" contained the notion of "bravado". It could, however, be used of things as well as persons, *e.g.* in his essay *Of Plantations*, Bacon says, "Iron is a *brave* commodity". It is still so used in certain phrases, *e.g.* "a *brave* show", "the *brave* new world" (the latter quoted from *The Tempest*). "Prettier" in the previous line has much the same sense.

between . . . boy, like a boy whose voice is breaking.

reed, like the sound of a reed instrument, *e.g.* an oboe.

quaint. See note on "quaintly order'd", p. 51.

I could not do withal, I could not do anything about it.

raw, clumsy, crude.

Jacks, jackanapes.

twenty miles. To the ferry. See note on "Padua", above. Apparently there were two routes between Venice and Belmont, one across the ferry and then by road, the other all the way by sea. It is rather curious that Bassanio waits for a favourable wind (II. vi. 64-5) when he could have gone at any time across the ferry and by road. Perhaps he thought that he would make more impression upon Portia if he went in his own ship instead of by "the common ferry".

Act III. Scene v

Jessica and Lorenzo are shown in control of Portia's establishment.

This scene gives an impression of the passing of time between Portia's decision to go to Venice in the previous scene and her arrival there in the following one.

Launcelot Gobbo's nonsense also provides a contrast with the deadly earnest of the trial-scene which follows.

fear you, fear *for* you. See note on "fear the enjoying", p. 59.

agitation. He means "*cog*itation" (malapropism).

Scylla. Charybdis. In classical story Scylla was a rock and Charybdis a whirlpool, the one on the Italian and the other near the Silician coast opposite. Sailors trying to shun the one fell in danger of the other.

gone, *i.e.* damned.

one by another, side by side, *i.e.* all trying to get a living together.

are out, have fallen out.

sirrah, fellow. Used rather contemptuously.

stomachs, appetites.

wit-snapper, snapper-up of words, in order to show your wit.

" cover ", lay the table.

Not so ... duty. Launcelot puns on the word "cover" and says that he will not cover his head before a superior. See note on "cover", p. 55.

quarrelling with occasion, taking the opportunity to twist words away from the sense in which they are meant.

meat, any kind of food, not just flesh. *Cf.* the phrase "*meat* and drink".

humours, moods, whims. *Cf.* Ben Jonson's play *Every Man in his Humour.*

dear discretion, complete discrimination (in choice of words). Lorenzo's comment is, of course, sarcastic.

suited, *i.e.* to his meaning.

stand in better place, are in a better position.

Garnish'd, furnished, set out (here with words).

Defy the matter, evade the meaning or the subject-matter.

How cheer'st thou. How are you? See note on "cheer", p. 63.

Past all expressing, more than I can say.

it, *i.e.* to "live an upright life".

there must be ... the other, *i.e.* "the other" would be so far inferior to Portia that something else would have to be thrown in with her to make the stakes equal. "Pawn'd" = pledged.

fellow, equal.

anon. This seems here to have the modern sense of soon or just now, rather than its usual Shakespearian sense (p. 50).

howso'er ... digest it, however uncomplimentary your opinion of me, it will not taste so bad digested with good food.

set you forth, show you what you are.

REVISION QUESTIONS ON ACT III

1. Show how Tubal increases Shylock's desire for revenge.

2. Show that Bassanio's avowed intention in wooing Portia gave place to something nobler while he was at Belmont.

3. Give Bassanio's comments on the caskets before he makes his choice, and state clearly why he chooses the leaden one.

4. Give Bassanio's description of Antonio to Portia. Was it justified?

5. What is Portia's plan to rescue Antonio?

ACT IV. SCENE I

This is the greatest scene in the play, indeed, one of the greatest in all literature. It is the struggle between villain and heroine. Antonio is up for trial, and owing to the difficulty of the case the Duke has sent for a learned doctor of laws to try it. In his absence, through sickness, comes Portia, bearing a letter of recommendation from him, posing as a doctor of laws, with Nerissa as her clerk. Shylock is deaf to all appeals for mercy. After giving him an opportunity to spare Antonio and take thrice the money due, just as he thinks he is sure of his case Portia turns the tables on him and defeats him with his own weapons. He had taken his stand on the letter of the law, and she keeps him to it. The bond said "a pound of flesh", therefore if he takes a fraction more or less than a pound or sheds one drop of blood he dies and his goods go to the state. Furthermore, the punishment for any alien found guilty of seeking the life of a citizen of Venice was to sacrifice half of his property to his intended victim and the other half to the state. Antonio undertakes to keep his half in trust for Lorenzo and Jessica, and at Antonio's suggestion the Duke remits the state's share providing Shylock makes that over to them on his death and also (the "most unkindest cut of all") becomes a Christian. No wonder that Shylock then feels unwell and asks permission to leave the court. Portia declines a reward, but after Bassanio's pressing her to reconsider it, asks him for his ring—the ring she had given him and he had sworn never to part with. Bassanio refuses, but after Portia has gone Antonio persuades him to change his mind, and he sends the ring after her by Gratiano.

Apart from the general character-contrast between Shylock and Portia, the grimness of the Jew's enmity is set off (and at the same time relieved) by some delightful touches of comic irony.

Magnificoes. See note p. 62.

your. thee. See note on "thee. thou", p. 43.

Uncapable. Un- and in- as negative prefixes could be used with the same root words in Elizabethan times.

qualify, modify, moderate. Antonio continues the Duke's metaphor in "dram of mercy" by using a word meaning modifying by mixing or blending.

that, since (that).

envy. See note on "envious plea of", p. 62.

very, utmost.

his, *i.e.* his spirit.

but lead'st . . . act, dost keep up this appearance of thy malice only to zero-hour (*i.e.* you will not act upon it).

remorse, pity.

where, whereas.

loose, give up, remit.

moiety, portion (Fr. "moitié" = half).

royal merchant. The very words used by Gratiano of Antonio in III. ii.

offices, actions. See note on "an office of discovery", p. 53.

possess'd. See note p. 45.

let the danger . . . freedom. See note on "Since . . . nations", p. 63. This is Shylock's trump card, as Salerio and Antonio have already realised (Act III, Scenes ii and iii respectively).

humour. See note p. 65.

is it answer'd? is that answer enough for you? The irritating repetition of the word "answer" in this speech (it occurs five times) emphasises that *this* is Shylock's reply to the Duke's appeal for "a gentle answer".

baned, destroyed, poisoned.

a gaping pig, either (1) a pig's head dressed for table with its mouth open, or (2) a squealing pig.

i' the nose, referring to the nasal tones of the bag-pipe.

affection, mistress of passion, our first reactions to outward stimuli ("affection") determine deep-seated inward feelings ("passion") to those particular things. For "affection" see also note on "The better . . . hopes", p. 38, and for "passion", p. 54.

sways . . . loathes. The first "it" refers to "passion", the second to "affection".

firm, sound.

he he. he. The men referred to in the passage seven lines above.

woollen. Referring to the cloth covering (the "bag" of) the bag-pipes.

of force, necessarily, *per*force.

offend, himself being offended, *i.e.* offend others, because he himself is offended by such things as I have named.

lodged, settled, deep-seated.

certain, fixed.   Much the same as "lodged".

A losing suit.   Because he will lose his money for the sake of worthless flesh.

current, course.   Metaphor from the flow of a river.

hate, cause of hatred.

offence, *i.e.* offence *taken.*

question, argue.

main flood, ocean.   Both words really have the same meaning.   See note on "flood", p. 38.

fretten, ruffled, blown to and fro.

judgment, *i.e.* my sentence.

draw.   As we speak of *drawing* money out of the bank.

abject, low, menial.

parts, positions, duties.   Perhaps a metaphor from acting a part in a play.

such, *i.e.* the same.

dearly bought.   Here bought by the sacrifice of his ducats.

answer.   It is Shylock's turn to ask for an answer.

Upon my power, by virtue of my authority.

determine, decide.

tainted, diseased.

hangman.   A term for all executioners.

inexecrable, one that cannot be cursed enough.

for thy life, that ever you are allowed to go on living.

To . . . Pythagoras, so as to share the opinion of Pythagoras. Pythagoras was a Greek philosopher who believed in the transmigration of souls.

trunks, bodies.   (Synecdoche.)

fell, cruel.

starved, murderous.   "To starve" used to mean to die by any means, not necessarily lack of food.

offend'st, injurest.   A stronger word than now.

cureless, incurable.

I stand here for law.   Five monosyllables with a punch in every one. Notice that but for three words this speech is entirely composed of monosyllables.

conduct, escort, guidance.   *Cf.* "safe-*conduct*".

at, at the time of.

in loving visitation, on a friendly visit.

Balthazar.   Portia had taken the name of her servant.

importunity, urgent request.

fill up, fulfil.

stead, place.   Not the same meaning as in "May you stead", note p. 44.

no impediment . . . esteem, no hindrance to his receiving reverence and esteem.

whose trial . . . commendation, your experience of his abilities will recommend him better (than my letter).

dressed like a doctor of laws.   In the garments obtained from Bellario (III. iv. 51-4).

difference, dispute.

holds, is the subject of.

such rule, so regular a form.

within his danger, in his power (and therefore in danger from him).

confess, acknowledge, admit.

strain'd, compelled, answering Shylock's question, "On what compulsion must I?" Mercy ceases to be mercy when it is forced, says Portia.

the mightiest, those who possess the greatest power (and are never "compelled"). *e.g.* monarchs.

shows, is the emblem of.

attribute to, symbol of. "Attribute" refers to "power" (not "sceptre").

Wherein . . . kings, in which rests the dread and fear in which kings are held.

sceptred sway, sway of the sceptre.

hearts. This word bears the emphasis—in the *hearts* not in the sceptre (symbolical of power) of kings.

seasons, tempers.

in the course of justice, if mere justice were given us.

bears down truth, overbears, crushes honesty.

Daniel. Not referring to the Daniel who was cast into the lions' den, but to the Daniel in *The Story of Susannah and the Elders,* one of the stories of the *Apocrypha.* When a young man (therefore corresponding to Portia in years) by a wise judgment he saved the woman Susannah, who had been falsely accused and condemned.

thrice. Actually Bassanio had offered Shylock only twice his principal, but perhaps Portia took it upon herself to increase it (after all it was her money) to see if by any means Shylock could be persuaded to "mitigate the justice of his plea".

the tenour, what is set forth in it.

Hath full relation, fully applies (to such a penalty as this).

more elder. Double comparatives and superlatives (*e.g.* "most unkindest") are quite frequent in Elizabethan literature.

his breast: so says the bond. Actually the terms of the bond suggested by Shylock in I. iii were that the flesh was to be taken "in what part your body pleaseth me". But perhaps the proviso that it was to be taken from his breast was put in at the notary's.

on your charge, at your own expense.

nominated, named, stated.

charity. See note p. 43.

arm'd. See ll. 11-13.

use. See note on "I do never use it", p. 46. Here a noun.

age, *i.e.* old age.

lingering penance of such misery, punishment of such lingering misery.

process, circumstances.

me fair in, well of me after.

Repent, grieve.

with all my heart. See note on "dam. damned", p. 57.

Your wife . . . offer. This episode brings in a delightful touch of comic irony into a tragic scene.

I have a daughter. Shylock was evidently going to say, "Whom I would not sacrifice" (as these *Christian* husbands are willing to sacrifice their wives), but then the memory of what she has done surges into his mind and he breaks off abruptly.

Barrabas. The criminal whom the Jews besought Pilate to release instead of Christ. See *Matthew*, xxvii. 15-26; *Mark*, xv. 6-15; *Luke*, xxiii. 13-25; *St. John*, xviii. 39-40.

trifle, waste.

rightful, righteous, "upright" as Gratiano says.

Come prepare! This is the climax of the scene. Shylock's hopes are now at their highest, but after this his fortunes steadily decline.

O upright judge! Gratiano flings back his own words into Shylock's teeth, not, however, with Shylock's bitterness, but with airy relief.

Soft! See note p. 45. Again, the irony is delightful when Portia intervenes to stop Bassanio getting rid of *her* money!

all, complete (according to the *letter* of the bond). See note p. 53.

just, exactly.

the substance . . . scruple, the whole or the fraction of a twentieth part of a mere scruple. This is the way the tables are turned on the man who specified "an *equal* pound" in his bond.

estimation, estimated weight.

have . . . hip. See note on "catch . . . hip", p. 45. Gratiano again uses words of Shylock, but here unconsciously.

principal. Shylock here moderates his demand to his principal. Before it was thrice the principal.

barely my principal, my bare principal.

so, *i.e.* in the way I have specified.

contrive, plot.

seize, take legal possession of. This speech of Portia's is cast in legal phraseology.

privy coffer, private treasury.

'gainst all other voice, in spite of the decision of anybody else.

manifest proceeding, plainly by the proceedings of the court.

formerly, aforesaid—another legal term.

rehearsed, pronounced.

general, public.

humbleness, your humility, "begging mercy".

drive, commute.

for, as for, *i.e.* the state has no jurisdiction over the half due to Antonio.

So, if it.

quit, remit. Antonio proposes that the state should exact nothing and that he himself should have the other half of Shylock's property only to keep in trust for Lorenzo and Jessica. Later on he adds that Shylock must make a will leaving the half he keeps to Lorenzo and Jessica.

use, trust.

record a gift, sign "a deed of gift". The force of "record" is that it shall be in writing.

I am not well. This need not be a pretence to get out of the court; Shylock had surely had enough to make him feel ill!

ten more, *i.e.* a jury of twelve.

your grace of pardon, pardon of your grace.
serves, permits.
gratify, reward.
in lieu whereof, in return for which.
freely cope, willingly requite.   Bassanio offers her her own money!
more mercenary, *i.e.* she has never wanted any further reward than the satisfaction of doing good.
know me . . . again.   A courteous farewell, something like, "Well, we may meet again", but a remark with special point spoken by Portia to Bassanio.
of force.   See note p. 67.
attempt you further, make a further attempt to persuade you.
tribute, acknowledgement.
pardon me, *i.e.* for my insistence.
for your love, as a token of your friendship.
it is a trifle!   Bassanio's pretext to keep the ring Portia had given him (Act III, Sc. ii, at the end of Portia's speech after he had chosen the right casket) leads him to call her ring a "trifle" to her face!
I have a mind to it, my mind is set on it.
taught me first to beg, *i.e.* persuaded me to take a reward when I did not want one.
methinks.   See note on "Methought", p. 45.
An if.   One of the words is redundant—they both have the same meaning.   See note on "An", p. 43.

Act IV.   Scene II

Gratiano overtakes Portia and gives her the ring, and in an aside to Portia Nerissa says that she will get Gratiano's ring, too.
Obviously, a similar ring incident is not repeated on the stage.

this deed.   The "deed of gift" he had undertaken to sign.
deed.   The deed above, not referring to their action in general.
well, very.
you are well o'erta'en, I am pleased to have overtaken you so quickly.
upon more advice, after further consideration.   See note on "be advised", p. 48.
That cannot be, *i.e.* she cannot accept the invitation.   In any case Portia could hardly accept Bassanio's invitation, having refused the Duke's.
mayst, wilt be able to.
old.   Intensifies the idea, *i.e.* plenty of; just as in familiar talk we say, "*Old* so and so".   *Cf.* "*old* Shylock", l. 11.
show, conduct.

REVISION QUESTIONS ON ACT IV

1. Who is the central figure in the trial-scene? Give reasons for your answer.

2. Give Shylock's reasons for following "a losing suit" against Antonio, and show clearly how Portia, after admitting Shylock's bond, turns the tables upon him.

3. What womanly qualities do you find in "Balthazar"?

4. Quote any moving speech from this Act.

5. Write a new scene entitled "Shylock's Home-coming", in which Tubal is there to receive him.

ACT V

Portia and Nerissa arrive home just before Bassanio, Antonio and Gratiano. Nerissa accuses Gratiano of giving her ring to a woman and this leads to the "discovery" that Bassanio also has given his ring away—to a woman, says Portia. After Bassanio's denials and explanations Portia presents him with the ring and the mystery is cleared up. The chatterbox has the last word.

This act provides a striking contrast to the scene in court. (*Cf.* Act III, Sc. v, and together the two scenes throw the trial-scene into strong relief between them.) There, in a stifling atmosphere, we saw the fierce rivalries of men. Here, in the open-air on a quiet moonlight night, we hear music and the beautiful language of happy lovers. It has already been noticed (p. 31) how a vivid impression of the moonlight setting is given at the start in the conversation of Lorenzo and Jessica, and thereafter is kept continuously before us by references to it at different points through the act by every important speaker except Antonio (who, indeed, speaks only a dozen lines in the whole act). The act ends in comedy arising from the pretended anger of Portia and Nerissa at their husbands' return without their rings. Everyone is happy and the past seems like a nightmare. Indeed, Professor Dover Wilson called this the happiest scene in all Shakespeare.

In this act all four plots are rounded off *together*, in one episode. Antonio, who had risked his life to help Bassanio win Portia as his wife, has in turn himself been delivered by that same wife. Lorenzo and Jessica are happy together after Jessica's flight from the Jew who had threatened Antonio, and are much better provided for as a result of his sentence. Finally, the ring episode, developing out of the trial, is happily cleared up.

in such a night. Notice how the alliteration of *s* and *z* sounds in this passage reproduces the sound of the wind "kissing the trees" (onomatopoeia).

Troilus. Son of Priam, King of Troy, in love with Cressida.

Troyan. Trojan.

Cressid. Deserted Troilus for the Greek Diomede. In medieval literature she stands for the faithless lover. The story is told in Shakespeare's play *Troilus and Cressida*.

lay, lodged, dwelt.

Thisbe. Arranged to meet her lover Pyramus, but while she was waiting for him a lioness approached, whereupon she fled, dropping her cloak, which the breast tore and stained with blood. When Pyramus came he saw Thisbe's blood-stained garment, imagined the worst and killed himself. On her return Thisbe found his dead body and she killed *herself*. The story forms the subject of the play within a play in Shakespeare's *A Midsummer Night's Dream*.

o'ertrip. In Elizabethan English it made little difference whether the preposition or adverb came before or after the verb, *e.g.* "my *down*sitting and my *up*rising".

ere himself, before (she saw the lion) himself.

Dido. Queen of Carthage. When Æneas called at Carthage she fell so deeply in love with him that on his departure she had herself burnt to death on a funeral pyre.

willow. An emblem of unhappy love.

waft, waved to.

Carthage. A famous city of the ancient world, situated at the northernmost part of the coast of Africa. See note on "Dido", above.

Medea ... enchanted ... Æson. Medea, the wife of Jason, renewed the youth of her husband's father, Æson, by a potion made from "enchanted herbs"—herbs gathered by moonlight to an incantation. See note on "Colchos. Jasons", p. 41.

unthrift, prodigal.

Stealing her soul. Jessica is humorously answering Lorenzo's charge that she "stole (a pun (1) stole away, (2) stole his ducats) from the wealthy Jew". You are as bad, she says, for you stole my soul.

In such a night did pretty Jessica. This brings it to the present. It was Jessica's previous speech which had "slandered her love".

out-night you, go one better than you in telling of things that happened "in such a night". Such compounds were common in Elizabethan English, *e.g.* outstare, outbrave (II. i. 27 and 28), outface, outswear (IV. ii. 17). We still have the words "outdo" and "outlast".

holy crosses, *i.e.* wayside shrines (common in Catholic countries). Portia had accounted to Lorenzo for her absence by saying that she was going to "a monastery two miles off" (III. iv. 31), not on a religious pilgrimage.

my master, *i.e.* Bassanio.

ceremoniously . . . welcome, let us prepare some ceremonious welcome. He arranges for music (l. 53) and lighting up the hall (l. 89).

Sola. Launcelot is imitating the "post's" "horn".

post. See note p. 56.

horn. A pun—(1) the messenger's horn to announce his arrival, (2) a horn as an emblem of plenty.

expect, await.

why should we go in? This avoids a change of scene.

signify, announce.

music, band of musicians. It was customary for the English nobles of Shakespeare's day to employ a private orchestra. In l. 55 the word has the modern meaning.

touches. The word suggests stringed instruments.

patines, small golden plates used in the celebration of the Eucharist in the Catholic Church.

in his motion . . . sings. The stars revolving in their spheres around the earth, regarded as fixed, were popularly supposed to make beautiful music, which, however, could not be heard by mortal ears ("this muddy vesture of decay").

quiring, singing in a choir. This is the usual spelling of the word "choir" throughout the seventeenth century.

cherubins. The plural of the Hebrew word "cherub" is "cherubim". The forms "cherubins" and "cherubims" (Authorised Version of the Bible) were due to a misunderstanding of a foreign plural, adding thereto the usual English plural termination -s.

this muddy vesture of decay, *i.e.* the body.

grossly close it in, coarsely and thickly enclose it (*i.e.* the harmony open to the soul, or perhaps the soul itself). For "close in" see note on "o'ertrip", p. 73.

Diana. See note p. 44. Here thought of as the goddess of the moon.

attentive, absorbed, engrossed. If the meaning is "You are thinking of something else", *we* should use "*in*attentive".

unhandled, not broken in.

Fetching, taking. Notice the onomatopoeia—the metre is altered in a line which speaks of "mad bounds".

mutual, with one consent.

modest, moderate (the usual meaning in Shakespeare's day). Here, perhaps, best rendered by "docile".

the poet. Ovid.

Orpheus. A famous musician who accompanied Jason in his quest for the golden fleece.

drew, *i.e.* so that they followed him—the same sense as in l. 68.

floods, rivers. Not the meaning of the singular in I. i. 10 and IV. i. 72.

nought, there is nought.

stockish, wooden (like the stump of a tree). "Stockish, hard, and full of rage" refer respectively to "trees, stones, and floods".

concord, harmony.

spoils, acts of plunder.

Erebus. In classical mythology a sort of no-man's-land between

Earth and Hell, through which the souls of the departed passed into Hades.

When the moon shone. Evidently there are clouds in the sky and it is not a clear moonlight night. *Cf.* l. 109.

brightly, as brightly.

empties itself, *i.e.* is swallowed up in the greater glory of his master.

main. See note on "main flood", p. 68.

respect, reference to circumstances. The light of the candle seems strong by itself, but pale against the moon, and similarly music sounds more beautiful in the silence of the night.

attended, paid any notice, listened to attentively. *Cf.* note on "attentive", p. 74.

by season . . . perfection, by coming at the right time are given their due praise and have their true excellence appreciated. There is a pun on "season", of course. *Cf.* note on "seasons", p. 69.

Endymion. A beautiful youth beloved of the moon goddess, who was so struck by his beauty that she came down to him and kissed him and lay by his side, and put him into an eternal sleep so that she might continue to visit him every night.

That is the voice. Lorenzo does not hear Portia until the music stops, and, of course, she would raise her voice to speak to the orchestra.

speed, prosper.

for our words. There is an ironic reference here to her words in the law-court.

tucket. A set of notes on a trumpet (see the next line).

We should . . . sun, we should have daylight at the same time as the people on the other side of the world if only *you* would walk during our night. Bassanio greets Portia with a graceful compliment—her presence is a sun in itself, no other is necessary.

light. See note p. 53.

heavy, *i.e.* heavy at heart.

sort all! see to everything, dispose of all.

bound. Portia puns on this word in her reply.

in all sense, in all reason, or perhaps in every respect.

acquitted of, freed from.

breathing courtesy. Exactly the same as "courteous breath"; see note on "breath", p. 56.

posy, motto. It was very fashionable in Shakespeare's time for wedding and engagement rings to be engraved on the inside with a motto. "Posy" is the same word as "poesy".

respective, careful. See notes on "respect upon", p. 40, and "with respect", p. 50.

an if. See note p. 71.

scrubbed, scrubby. The humour of this conversation consists in the dramatic irony, where Gratiano denies Nerissa's charge that he gave her ring to a woman, and then goes on in very uncomplimentary language to describe the "boy" to whom he gave it—"a little scrubbed boy, *no higher than thyself!*"

so slightly, on so slight an excuse.

leave it, part with it, let it go. *Cf.* l. 150.

masters, is master of, possesses.

I were best. See note on "You were best", p. 54.

If you did know. The repetition in these lines—consisting almost entirely of monosyllables—gives force to what Bassanio says.

virtue, power (Lat. "virtus").

your . . . contain the ring, how your own honour was involved in retaining the ring.

man. No doubt Portia would teasingly emphasise this word.

terms, words, expressions.

wanted . . . ceremony? (as to have) lacked good manners so much as to press for a thing regarded as a sacred emblem?

civil doctor, doctor of civil law.

shame and courtesy, shame at acting discourteously.

candles of the night, *i.e.* stars.

liberal. See note p. 50.

enforced, forced on me, which I could not help.

double. Punning on the meaning "double-dealing".

of credit, worthy of being believed.

wealth, welfare. *Cf.* "common*wealth*".

Which. The antecedent is "body", not "wealth".

soul. Emphasised, *i.e.* with my *soul*, not my *flesh*, as a forfeit this time.

advisedly, deliberately. See note on "upon more advice", p. 71.

amazed, thunderstruck. A stronger word then than now.

argosies. See note p. 38.

suddenly, unexpectedly.

living. See note p. 61.

road. See note p. 39.

satisfied . . . full, fully satisfied concerning these events.

charge . . . inter'gatories, ask us questions to be answered on oath "Inter'gatories" (interrogatories) is a legal term.

Revision Questions on Act V

1. *The Merchant of Venice* is sometimes played without Act V (ending at IV. i). What is your opinion of this?

2. Show how this Act presents a marked contrast to the trial scene.

3. What does Lorenzo say about "the sweet power of music"?

4. Give a short account of the complication produced by the return of Bassanio and Gratiano without their rings.

5. By what means is the atmosphere of Belmont created? Refer to (*a*) the action, (*b*) the setting, and (*c*) the dialogue of this scene.

QUESTIONS
GENERAL QUESTIONS

1. "Although the play takes its title from Antonio, Shylock is the central character" (p. 13). Can you think of a better title than *The Merchant of Venice*? If so, justify it.

2. Imagine that you are a newspaper correspondent and that your day's assignment is Shylock's suit against Antonio in the court of Venice. Write your report.

3. Tell the story of Lorenzo and Jessica in so far as you can detach it from the rest of the play.

4. Tell what happened to the rings that Portia and Nerissa gave to their husbands, and say why you think Shakespeare introduced this episode into the play.

5. Show carefully how Shakespeare has interwoven four different stories or incidents in this play.

6. What are the points of contact between the Bond-story and the Caskets-story?

7. If you wished to shorten the acting-time of *The Merchant of Venice*, which scenes would you cut out? Give the reasons for your choice.

8. Could any minor character be omitted without taking away from the play anything essential?

9. What can be said in excuse of Shylock?

10. For a long time Shylock was represented on the stage as a grotesque monster. Justify the modern interpretation of his character.

11. Do you consider that Shylock got justice by Portia's verdict? Whatever conclusion you come to, give your reasons.

12. What effect upon Shylock has (*a*) the flight of Jessica, (*b*) Tubal's way of presenting the reports of her extravagance?

13. What traits in Portia's character are revealed (*a*) when she passes her suitors in review and discusses her father's will with Nerissa, (*b*) when she hears of Antonio's arrest, and (*c*) at the trial of Shylock?

14. Nearly all the characters in *The Merchant of Venice* admire Portia. Do you? Give reasons for your answer.

15. Is Bassanio worthy of (*a*) Portia as a wife, (*b*) Antonio as a friend? State for what reasons.

16. Portia said that true friends have "a like proportion of lineaments, of manners, and of spirit". Is this true of Antonio and Bassanio?

17. Do you find Antonio an attractive character? State the reasons for your answer.

18. Contrast the way in which Shylock and Antonio look upon the sudden loss of their accumulated wealth.

19. Give a short character of Gratiano and indicate his part in the action of the play.

20. Compare and contrast the characters of (*a*) Bassanio and Gratiano, (*b*) Antonio and Gratiano, supporting your answer by quotation.

21. Who wins the best wife, Bassanio, Gratiano or Lorenzo? Give full reasons for your answer.

22. Do you think that the marriage of Gratiano and Nerissa will turn out happily? Upon what do you base your decision?

23 Show the importance of the part taken in the play by *three* of the following, and briefly state their chief characteristics: (*a*) Nerissa, (*b*) Lorenzo, (*c*) Jessica, (*d*) Launcelot Gobbo.

24. How are the characters of Morocco and Arragon shown up by their speeches?

25. Mention two places in the play where prose is the medium and suggest reasons for its use in each case.

QUESTIONS ON THE TEXT

1. Thou art too wild, too rude and bold of voice;
Parts that become thee happily enough,
And in such eyes as ours appear not faults;
But where thou art not known, why, there they show
Something too liberal. Pray thee, take pain
To allay with some cold drops of modesty
Thy skipping spirit, lest, through thy wild behaviour,

I be misconstru'd in the place I go to,
And lose my hopes.

    (a) What made Bassanio draw attention to Gratiano's faults at this particular moment?

    (b) For what other faults does he at any time condemn him? State the occasion.

    (c) Does he ever say anything in praise of him?

    (d) Mention one other quality or talent that Gratiano possesses that Bassanio nowhere refers to and give an instance when it is shown.

    (e) Can you account for Bassanio's addressing Gratiano as "thou"?

2. The duke cannot deny the course of law:
For the commodity that strangers have
With us in Venice, if it be denied,
Will much impeach the justice of the state;
Since that the trade and profit of the city
Consisteth of all nations.

    (a) Explain in your own words why "The duke cannot deny the course of law".

    (b) Mention two other people who realise this besides Antonio.

    (c) What is the meaning of (i) commodity, (ii) impeach?

3. How sweet the moonlight sleeps upon this bank!
Here will we sit, and let the sounds of music
Creep in our ears: soft stillness and the night
Become the touches of sweet harmony.
Sit, Jessica: look, how the floor of heaven
Is thick inlaid with *patines* of bright gold:
There's not the smallest orb which thou behold'st
But in his motion like an angel sings,
Still quiring to the young-eyed *cherubins*;
Such harmony is in immortal souls;
But whilst *this muddy vesture of decay*
Doth grossly *close it in*, we cannot hear it.

    (a) What occasioned Lorenzo's speaking of music on this occasion?

    (b) Explain in your own words the popular belief to which allusion is made in the second half of this passage.

    (c) Give the meaning of the words in italics.

    (d) Mention any other occasion in the play when music is mentioned or heard.

4. Nor is the wide world ignorant of her worth,
For the four winds blow in from every coast
Renowned suitors; and her sunny locks
Hang on her temples like a golden fleece;
Which makes her seat of Belmont Colchos' strand,
And many Jasons come in quest of her.
O my Antonio! had I but the means
To hold a rival place with one of them,
I have a mind presages me such thrift,
That I should questionless be fortunate.

    (*a*) Explain the comparison with the "golden fleece" and the allusion to "Colchos' strand" and "Jasons".

    (*b*) What is the meaning of the last line but one?

    (*c*) What purpose has Bassanio in praising the lady at this moment?

5. *Gratiano*. A second Daniel, a Daniel, Jew!
Now, infidel, I have thee on the hip.
    Portia. Why doth the Jew pause? take thy forfeiture.
    Shylock. Give me my principal, and let me go.
    Bassanio. I have it ready for thee; here it is.
    Portia. He hath refused it in the open court:
He shall have merely justice and his bond.
    Gratiano. A Daniel still say I, a second Daniel!—
I thank thee, Jew, for teaching me that word.
    Shylock. Shall I not have barely my principal?

    (*a*) What occasions Gratiano's reference to "a Daniel"? Explain the allusion.

    (*b*) What does he mean by "I have thee on the hip"? Refer to an earlier occasion when Shylock used the same metaphor.

    (*c*) "Why doth the Jew pause?" Answer this question.

    (*d*) What was the "principal"? What offer had Bassanio made earlier with reference to this "principal"?

    (*e*) In what tones of voice do you imagine Gratiano and Shylock to speak?

6. Well, well: but, for mine own part, as I have set up my rest to run away, so I will not rest till I have run some ground. My master's a very Jew: give him a present! give him a halter: I am famished in his service; you may tell every finger I have with my ribs. Father, I am glad you

are come: give me your present to one Master Bassanio, who, indeed, gives rare new liveries. If I serve not him, I will run as far as God has any ground.

    (a) Why has Launcelot "set up his rest to run away"? Explain the phrase.

    (b) This conversation between Launcelot and his father leads to another interview. With whom and with what result?

    (c) Why is this speech in prose?

    (d) What is the *dramatic* purpose of the incident in which these words occur?

    (e) Have you any comment to make on "as far as God has any ground"?

7.   Well, Jessica, go in:
Perhaps I will return immediately:
Do as I bid you; shut doors after you:
"Fast bind, fast find,"
A proverb never stale in thrifty mind.

    (a) What is the *dramatic* reason for Shylock's uncertainty about his movements?

    (b) *Did* he "return immediately"?

    (c) What did Jessica do while he was away?

    (d) Comment on the short line, and the rhyme in the last two lines.

8. There are a sort of men, whose visages
Do cream and mantle like a standing pond,
And do a wilful stillness entertain,
With purpose to be dress'd in an opinion
Of wisdom, gravity, profound conceit;
As who should say, "I am Sir Oracle,
And when I ope my lips, let no dog bark!"
O my Antonio, I do know of these
That therefore only are reputed wise
For saying nothing.

    (a) Give the meaning of the passage as simply as possible in your own words.

    (b) What do you think was Gratiano's purpose in uttering these remarks at this point?

    (c) Point out any figures of speech in the passage.

9. If you prick us, do we not bleed? if you tickle us, do we not laugh? if you poison us, do we not die? and if you

wrong us, shall we not revenge? If we are like you in the rest, we will resemble you in that. If a Jew wrong a Christian, what is his humility? Revenge. If a Christian wrong a Jew, what should his sufferance be by Christian example? Why, revenge. The villany you teach me, I will execute, and it shall go hard but I will better the instruction.

(a) Is there any occasion *in the play* where a Christian shows a revengeful spirit?

(b) Explain "sufferance", "it shall go hard but I will better the instruction".

(c) Does Shylock "better the instruction"?

(d) Say *briefly* how far you think that the Christians are responsible for Shylock's malice.

10. These be the Christian husbands! I have a daughter,—
Would any of the stock of Barabbas
Had been her husband rather than a Christian!
We trifle time; I pray thee, pursue sentence.

(a) What had "the Christian husbands" just said or done to occasion this outburst?

(b) Why do you think that Shylock breaks off at "daughter"?

(c) Was it natural that his daughter should marry against his wish?

(d) Do you think that she would be happy with her Christian husband? Why?

(e) "I pray thee, pursue sentence." Why does Shylock *particularly* wish to get on with the business in hand at this moment?

11. Why, yet it lives there unchecked that Antonio hath a ship of rich lading wrecked on the narrow seas; the Goodwins, I think they call the place; a very dangerous flat and fatal, where the carcasses of many a tall ship lie buried, as they say, if my gossip Report be an honest woman of her word.

(a) "It lives there." Where?

(b) What is the importance of this news (or rumour) for the chief people in the play?

(c) Comment on "the Goodwins, *I think they call the place*".

(f) Explain the meaning of "it lives there unchecked", "of rich lading".

12. How like a fawning publican he looks!
I hate him for he is a Christian;

But more, for that in low simplicity
He lends out money gratis, and brings down
The rate of usance here with us in Venice.
If I can catch him once upon the hip,
I will feed fat the ancient grudge I bear him.
He hates our sacred nation, and he rails
Even there where merchants most do congregate
On me, my bargains, and my well-won thrift,
Which he calls interest.   Cursed be my tribe,
If I forgive him!

    (*a*) What is "a fawning publican", "low simplicity"?

    (*b*) Show briefly what two traits of Shylock's character are shown by his view of Antonio.

    (*c*) This speech was spoken "aside".   Who else was present on the stage when Shylock made it?

(Where no line is given, it is owing to the interposition of prose in the scene and consequent variation of numbering in different editions.)

(1) II. ii, (2) III. iii. 26-31, (3) V. 54-65, (4) I. i. 168-77, (5) IV. i. 334-43, (6) II. ii, (7) II. v. 51-5, (8) I. i. 88-97, (9) III. i, (10) IV. i. 296-9, (11) III. i. 2-7, (12) I. iii.

PASSAGES SUGGESTED FOR MEMORISING

I. i. 22-40, 79-102, 161-76; iii, Shylock's speech (aside) beginning "How like a fawning publican he looks!" and the one beginning "Signior Antonio, many a time and oft".

II. i. 1-7; ii, Bassanio's last long speech, beginning at "But hear thee, Gratiano"; iii. 1-4; vi. 8-19; viii. 35-49; ix. 90-4.

III. i, Shylock's speech immediately before "Enter a Servant", "Hath not a Jew eyes? . . . we will resemble you in that"; ii. 73-88, 149-65, and Bassanio's speech beginning "The dearest friend to me"; iv. 10-23, 62-78.

IV. i. 17-62, 70-83, Portia's speech beginning "The quality of mercy" as far as "The deeds of mercy", and the one beginning "He is well paid that is well satisfied" as far as "Never yet more mercenary".

V. 1-6, 54-65, 83-8.